Fighting Mustang:
Chronicle of the P-51

William N. Hess
Historian of the
American Fighter Aces Association

Library of Congress Cataloging in Publication Data

Hess, William N.
    Fighting Mustang.

    Reprint. Originally published: Garden City, N.Y.: Doubleday, 1970.
    Includes index.
    1. Mustang (Fighter planes) I. Title.
UG1242.F5H47   1985   358.4'3   85-5904
ISBN: 0-912173-04-1

ACKNOWLEDGMENTS

Many years of intensive research in the field of fighter planes and aces spawned the idea for this book. The encouragement of Mr. Stanley M. Ulanoff, more research and many people have made it possible.

Lt. Col. Robert A. Webb, Chief, Book Branch of the Office of the Assistant Secretary of Defense, opened the doors to the official records, and Miss Margo Kennedy and the wonderful staff of Aerospace Studies Institute left no stone unturned to make these records available to me.

Mr. J. L. Typer and Mr. D. B. Wright of North American Rockwell Corporation dug deeply into the records at the home of the Mustang to make them available. Mr. Gerald Tyler and Cavalier Aircraft Corporation brought the history of the Mustang up to date.

Wartime Mustang pilots furnished invaluable assistance from their excellent memories of those days. To these veteran pilots my heartfelt thanks: Lt. Col. Richard E. Turner, Ret., M/Gen. Edward B. Giller, Col. Sidney S. Woods, Ret., Dr. Clayton K. Gross, Mr. Kenneth H. Dahlberg, Mr. Jim Brooks, Mr. Fred Holmes, S/Ldr. F. E. Dymond, Mr. J. B. Walton, Jr., Mr. Wendell Hook, Col. Bert W. Marshall, Jr., Ret., Col. William T. Whisner, Ret., and Lt. Col. Robert Goebel, Ret.

Deepest appreciation to the late Grover C. Hall for his co-operation and assistance. My fine English aviation historians Mr. Chris Shores and Mr. Roger C. Freeman came through with vital information in their usual wonderful manner.

Many of the excellent and rare photos in this book came from private collections. The generosity of these men is unexcelled: Mr. R. C. Jones, Mr. Richard M. Hill, Mr. Bill Marshall, Mr. Albert H. Meryman, T/Sgt. David W. Menard, Mr. Ernie McDowell, Mr. Robert M. Gers, Mr. David Weatherill, Mr. Kenn C. Rust, Mr. Ralph R. Howard and Mr. Earl Reinert.

Finally, to my wife Ann, my deepest gratitude for her patience through the trials and tribulations of putting these pages together.

CONTENTS

APPENDIX

CHAPTER 1

THE COLT

The Mustang does not owe its birth to the U. S. Army Air Force with which it gained its greatest fame. Nor can it be said that its conception was made possible by the British Air Purchasing Commission. This design became reality due to the foresight and determination of one man — James H. "Dutch" Kindelberger.

As early as 1938, Kindelberger had made numerous trips to Europe seeking aircraft orders for his young North American Aviation Company, and there he had the opportunity to observe the airplanes which would see their initial combat in 1939. After hostilities broke out in Europe, Kindelberger eagerly sought reports of aircraft performance from observers in the combat arena. From this information, ideas of his own were developed that would bear lasting benefits to the Allies in the years to come.

In April of 1940, Kindelberger was summoned by the British Air Purchasing Commission and requested to put into production in his plant the Curtiss P-40 for use by the Royal Air Force.

Well aware of the limitations of the P-40 and anxious to put his own ideas into action, Kindelberger replied, "Hell, we can do better than that airplane and design you a real one in the same time it will take to put this thing in production."

Serious doubts were expressed, but the British were willing to give him the opportunity. Kindelberger returned to his plant in California, and showing great faith in his design team, presented the challenge. Edgar Schmued and Raymond Rice went to work immediately to come up with a prototype. Relying heavily on the axiom, "You can't pull a rabbit out of a hat unless you carefully put a rabbit into the hat beforehand," Kindelberger demanded the best from his engineers, and he got it. Customary design procedure was forgotten. Design data, including wind tunnel tests which Curtiss had done on an advanced P-40 design, was immediately rushed to men who were preparing the wooden mock-up of the airplane in the experimental shop. A $20,000 laminated-mahogany scale model was prepared for wind-tunnel tests in record time, yet tolerances were measured down to .001 of an inch.

The original Mustang, NA-73, prototype of the P-51. This aircraft may be seen at the Experimental Aircraft Association in Wisconsin. (North American)

In a drab room over Kindelberger's office, the design team knew no hours. The lights never went out and the average day was at least 16 hours long.

Several innovations marked the design for success. One was the laminar-flow wing which, with its maximum thickness well aft, resulted in greatly reduced drag which in turn made possible greater speed for given horsepower. The National Advisory Committee for Aeronautics had developed this high-lift, low-drag airfoil, but most engineers were of the opinion that it was too revolutionary and unproved to be incorporated into a mass-produced aircraft. North American's team decided to give it a try, but promised to come up with a conventional wing within 30 days should the test fail.

When the first wind-tunnel tests were run at California Institute of Technology, it seemed that the laminar flow wing had not lived up to expectations. Stall characteristics were bad. Quickly and carefully the airfoil was modified and brought back, but once again the wing didn't check out satisfactorily. Then the engineers suspected that the model was too large for the tunnel; the walls were affecting the airflow at the wing tips. The model was then flown to the University of

Washington at Seattle, where a larger tunnel was available. Here the wing passed all its tests with flying colors!

The radiator for the Allison engine was positioned aft of the cockpit with a further drag-eliminating narrow intake. Here, too, difficulties were encountered, as turbulence tended to build up under the wing, which prevented a clean flow of air into the scoop. This was remedied by dropping the entrance an inch. This proved sufficient to bypass the disturbed air under the wing. Once this was accomplished, the design enjoyed the smallest and most drag-free cross-sectional area placed behind any American-built inline engine.

North American further differentiated from all other Allied designers in incorporating square wing tips and tail surfaces. From the first day forward, the Mustang truly possessed the lines of a champion.

Delay in delivery of the Allison V-1710-39 prevented the first flight until October 26, 1940, although the prototype was rolled out on borrowed wheels in approximately 125 days. Test pilot Vance Breese took up the shiny new aircraft, designated NA-73S, that fall day and reportedly praised its performance. The Colt was born!

The first production NA-73 was retained at North American for testing purposes, but the second craft went to England, where it arrived in November of 1941. There it was dubbed the Mustang Mark I. This new fighter gained quick recognition

The second XP-51 undergoing evaluation at Wright Field, serial number 41-039. (USAF Museum)

as the best aircraft yet delivered from America, although it was handicapped by its low-altitude-rated Allison engine. On the other hand, it was highly maneuverable, and its internal fuel capacity of 150 imperial gallons gave it a range potential far surpassing that of any fighters on duty with the Royal Air Force. It possessed a heavy armament of four .50-caliber and two .30-caliber machine guns, which provided great strafing capability. These features suggested its use for tactical reconnaissance and ground support.

On the strength of its performance in the testing program, the first British contract called for 320 of the new fighters, with the proviso that two of the machines be delivered to the U. S. Army Air Corps for evaluation. These two aircraft, the fifth and tenth production NA-73s, were designated XP-51s.

The Mustangs delivered under the original contract differed little from the original model other than that an F-24 camera had been mounted behind the pilot. It was in a ground-support configuration that the Mustang entered service with the Royal Air Force Army Co-operation Squadrons.

The first unit to receive the aircraft was No. 26 Squadron, which began augmenting its Curtiss Tomahawks with the new fighter in February 1942. In April, two more squadrons were so equipped and a further eight squadrons received Mustang Is during June.

A Mustang Mark I with the K-24 camera behind the cockpit. (RAF)

Number 26 Squadron took the Mustang I on its first operational sortie on July 27, 1942. But the new fighter received its baptism of fire during the Dieppe raid by British commandos on August 19. On this day, pilots of No. 414 RCAF Squadron were attacked over the port city by FW 190s. During this fight, Flying Officer H. H. Hills downed one of the enemy. First blood for the Mustang!*

On the same day, Pilot Officer C. H. Stover, while flying wingman on a deep reconnaissance, was attacked by a low-flying Focke-Wulf. In the course of violent evasive action on the deck, Stover ran into a telephone pole and lost three feet from the tip of his starboard wing. Despite this, he managed to bring the Mustang home to England where he made a crash landing.

The first announcement of the long-range capability of the Mustang appeared in English newspapers during October of 1942 and read as follows: ''The Mustangs — American-built and the fastest co-operational aircraft in the world — had for their targets the Dortmund-Ems Canal and objectives in Holland. They made a round trip of between 600 and 700 miles. . .''

On this mission the Mustang I became the first single-engined fighter based in the United Kingdom to penetrate the German border. The Mustangs opened their

*Hills added four victories in 1944 while flying F6F Hellcats in the U.S. Navy; perhaps the rarest achievement of any American ace.

Number 2 Squadron RAF flew Mustang Is from 1942 into 1944. (Cook via Jones)

attack just before crossing the German-Dutch frontier, when they strafed a military camp while flying right on the deck. Then, in the Dortmund-Ems Canal, they swept down on a factory and gas depot at Lathen. Continuing along the canal, they scored hits on several barges and left a 500-ton ship burning in the Zuyder Zee.

The Royal Air Force was so pleased with the Mustang I that it placed an order for 300 more, which embodied only minor modifications. Subsequently another 150 fighters were ordered, which called for the machine guns to be replaced by four 20mm cannon. This was in keeping with the Royal Air Force policy at that time, attempting to increase the firepower of its fighters. These cannon-armed craft were designated NA-91 by North American and Mustang Mark IA by the Royal Air Force.

However, the British never received all of the aircraft manufactured under this contract for 150 Mustangs. Fifty-five NA-91s were delivered to the U. S. Army Air Force armed with four .50-caliber machine guns rather than cannon and fitted

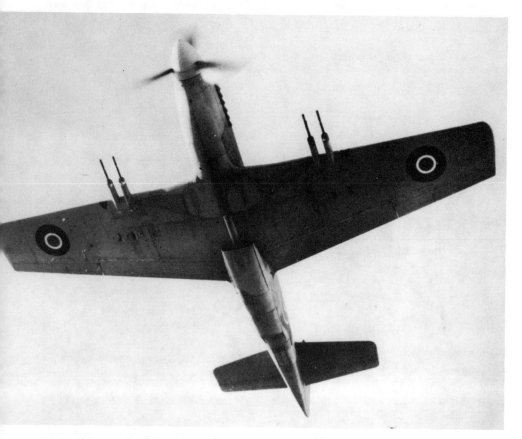

An in-flight view of the Mustang IA showing the formidable arament of twin 20mm cannon in each wing. (RAF)

"Slick Chick" was the second of 310 P-51As (serial 43-6004) which featured four .50 caliber guns and A-36 bomb racks without the dive brakes. (USAF Museum)

with two K-24 cameras. These aircraft were designated tactical reconnaissance planes and were typed F-6As by the Army Air Force. They were originally called Apache, but this Indian tribal name didn't stick, and in only a few months the United States forces chose to call the aircraft by its British title — Mustang. A number of F-6As saw action in North Africa during the Tunisian campaign.

At the time of testing the Mustang in Great Britain, Major Thomas Hitchcock was serving as the U. S. Military Attache in London, and this veteran pilot was swept up with the early success and performance of the aircraft. In the fall of 1942 he informed Washington that the Mustang was by far the best fighter airframe developed to date, but in view of the shortcoming of the Allison engine, he proposed a marriage of the North American airframe with the Rolls-Royce Merlin 61 engine. His opinion was seconded by others, including RAF Air Marshal Sir Stafford Leigh-Mallory. Four Mustangs were delivered to the Rolls-Royce factory for modification.

A Mustang Mark I received a Merlin 65 and a Mustang IA was modified to take a Merlin 61 and both were fitted with four-bladed propellers. During testing, a further two airplanes were fitted with Merlins and designated Mustang Xs. The flight tests were amazing and so impressed all concerned that North American decided to redesign the aircraft to take a Packard-built Merlin, the V-1650-3, with two-speed, two-stage supercharger and intercooler.

Two P-51s were equipped with the Packard-built engines at the California plant for testing and for a time carried the designation of XP-78s, but this soon gave way to XP-51B. The airframes were beefed up, the carburetor intake was moved from above to below the nose, and underwing racks were installed to take two 1000-pound bombs or long-range fuel drop tanks.

The high-altitude performance and increase in level speed of the new Mustang to 441 mph were enough to really sell the USAAF on the little fighter, and an initial order of 2200 Merlin-powered P-51Bs was placed with North American.

Meanwhile, pilots of the Royal Air Force Co-operation Command continued to do yeoman duty over occupied countries of Europe. Bombing, strafing and tactical

A glimpse of the future. This early P-51B was apparently reclaimed from a British batch and retained for evaluation. The Merlin-powered Mustang is seen low over the oil fields of southern California. (USAF Museum)

reconnaissance comprised the bulk of their missions. A favorite with the pilots was train busting. A young South African pilot reported, "I flew over one engine pulling thirty cars and gave it a squirt. Then I went on down the line, got another just about to go under a bridge. The engine did not burst, but it was just as if you had put a lot of holes suddenly in a tin can. Steam blew all over the place."

Such activities placed quite a strain on the German-operated railroads. Engines had to be armored and flak guns were placed on flatcars, but the measures were never enough. During this period passenger trains were strictly "taboo" due to the large number of friendly civilians occupying the coaches, but if a pilot got a good crack at the locomotive, the train was apt to run late.

Royal Air Force pilots were not only pleased with the excellent performance of the Mustang, but with its ability to take punishment and come home. "The sturdiness of these splendid U. S. fighters is wonderful," one British pilot testified. "Some of them have taken punishment which would have been too much for most fighters. One of them, which was getting a particularly hot time from enemy ack-ack, had a bullet in his ammunition box. This blew up a number of cartridges, as a result of which the Mustang was simply riddled with splinters.

"The wing was damaged and the pilot wounded, but he got the aircraft home and landed it safely."

Wing Commander Peter Dudjeon, former squadron leader of an RAF Army Co-operation unit, praised the Mustang Is and IAs.

"The long range of this aircraft made it an excellent tactical reconnaissance aircraft and its armament made it effective against most ground targets. As their operations progressed, they swung more and more to offensive reconnaissance and began to take advantage of targets of opportunity until the operation finally developed into a strategic effort against ground objectives such as railway locomotives, canal barges, heavy motor transport and aircraft on the ground.

"These daylight intrusion raids (rhubarbs) were very successful, largely due to the care and effort which went into the planning and operations of their missions. The theme was the destruction of those targets designated with the minimum number of casualties. That this was achieved is attested by the record of this squadron which in eighteen months of operations destroyed or damaged severely, 200 locomotives, over 200 barges and an undetermined number of enemy aircraft on the ground. This was accomplished with only one Mustang being shot down by enemy fighters, five planes lost to enemy flak and two vanished without record as to their fate. During this period of operations, they were never once intercepted over enemy territory. This included raids over Holland, occupied France, Belgium and Germany, the longest one having been a flight over 1000 miles. Their furthermost victory was a locomotive shot up just outside Wilhelmshaven, an airline distance of approximately 350 miles from their base.

"It has been found that the Mustang is faster than the Me 109 and the FW 190 and that 4000 to 8000 feet is a good altitude at which to catch the enemy. At sea level, the Mustang can run away from any enemy aircraft they have encountered to date. The pilots are schooled to run rather than fight, because their main object is the destruction of ground targets, not to fight enemy aircraft. They are instructed in the use of flaps in combat to reduce their turning radius. At least one FW 190 has been made to spin in through the use of a small amount of flap by the Mustang then engaged in a turning contest at low altitude. The 190 tried to tighten his turn to keep the Mustang in his sights after the pilot had dropped his flaps slightly, but spun out of the turn."

One Mustang pilot who decided to mix it up a bit was Pilot Officer R. P. Bethell of 268 Squadron, flying with a four-plane patrol off Snailwell on the afternoon of November 26, 1942. Bethell saw an Me-109F at 1500 feet so he climbed to the attack and fired a four-second burst at 250 yards, seeing strikes. He closed and fired another burst at 200 yards, rapidly closing to point-blank range. The 109 burst into flames and crashed. Shortly after this encounter he saw a Junkers 52 transport lumbering along the coast at 500 feet. Attacking immediately, he let fly with a long burst and continued to fire while closing the gap from 300 to 50 yards. The Junkers poured heavy smoke, crashed and exploded.

Pilots of the Royal Canadian Air Force inaugurated night intruder missions with Mustangs in the spring of 1943. On the night of April 13, Pilot Officer Peters and Flying Officer F. M. Grant took off and set course for the darkened skies of France to seek their prey. This evening, luck would be with them. In the Paris area, Grant found night-flying training taking place. Stealthfully he closed in on the tail of a Dornier 217, gave him a short squirt of lead and saw him crash in a ball of fire. With all guns of the installation now alerted, the two pilots went "balls out" for home.

Flying Officer F. E. Hanton had one of the Canadians' better nights intruding in a Mustang. Roaring over the French countryside, Hanton spotted a train in motion near Vire and dived on it with all guns blazing. The locomotive absorbed a lethal dose and clouds of steam rose in the summer darkness as the train came to an abrupt halt.

Continuing on to the Rennes airdrome, the Mustng pilot sighted several enemy aircraft in the landing pattern of the lit-up field. Just what he had been waiting for! Immediately he lined up a Junkers 88 and gave it a good burst. The German pilot instantly cut his navigation lights and went into a dive. The brilliant flash of his guns served as just enough of a blinder to make Hanton lose his target.

Continuing his nocturnal quest, Hanton next sighted a Messerschmitt 110 on final approach. Diving down, the Canadian gave the Luftwaffe craft a short burst and watched it dive right on into the ground. As he pulled up over his victim,

Hanton found himself in the middle of intense flak and probing searchlight fingers. Diving for the deck, he headed for home.

Mustang Is and IAs saw combat with the Royal Air Force up until 1944, and as the records attest, performed magnificently. The days of conquest over the Luftwaffe at high altitude came later with the Merlin-powered models, but as a low-altitude, interdiction and reconnaissance aircraft, the early Mustang knew few equals. Truly, the pony from North American had won its spurs.

CHAPTER 2

THE INVADER

In the spring of 1942 a new version of the P-51A was evolved specifically for dive-bombing. This model was fitted with wing-mounted air brakes, a 1325 h.p. Allison V-1710-87 engine, and was designated the A-36A. Five hundred A-36s were built for the AAF, but the majority of its combat was centered around two fighter-bomber groups in the Mediterranean Theater of Operations — the 27th and the 86th.

Both units arrived in North Africa in the late spring of 1943, just after the close of the Tunisian campaign, and saw their first action during the reduction by air of the island of Pantelleria. The men of the A-36s had been told in the United States that their dive brakes would be all but useless and the best thing to do was to wire them closed. This proved an incorrect appraisal, and they were used throughout the Sicilian campaign and the Italian invasion with great success.

Not only was the A-36 a fine dive-bombing aircraft, it proved a very stable and effective ground strafer. The quietness of its engine enabled it to get right on top of ground targets before the enemy realized it was in the vicinity, and the scream of the dive flaps gained the A-36 the name of "screaming helldivers" by the Germans.

The A-36 was known to American forces as the Invader and it really lived up to its name, for it was to see yeoman service during both the invasion of Sicily and of Italy. During the Sicilian campaign the airplane proved itself and gained the everlasting praise of the pilots who flew it.

Dive-bombing was usually carried out from an altitude of approximately 10,000 to 12,000 feet. The A-36s would break into single file and make their dive-bombing runs in trail. Bombing speed would be held to around 290-300 miles per hour when the dive brakes were fully extended. Bombs were dropped at about 3000 feet and pullout was accomplished at approximately 1500 feet. Bombing was very accurate, and it wasn't unusual for hits to stack up on top of the target.

The A-36 carried six .50-caliber machine guns, two firing through the propeller and two in each wing. For their primary mission of ground strafing, the Invader

An A-36A in olive-drab warpaint. The Invader proved an excellent dive-bomber and close-support aircraft, despite vulnerability of its liquid-cooled Allison engine. (USAF)

Photo-recon P-51s were redesignated F-6As and introduced to USAAF operations in the Mediterranean Theater. This "snooper" flew with the 68th Reconnaissance Group in 1943.

pilots usually had their guns synchronized to concentrate their fire at 200-250 yards. The impact of such a force was enough to bring about the destruction of almost anything they encountered on the ground.

As a ground strafer, the A-36 could take it and still come home. One lieutenant was returning from a mission on the west coast of Italy when he sighted a staff car traveling along at high speed. He made a sharp diving turn, and at such a steep angle it was difficult to judge the terrain. As he concentrated on his target, he got a little low and went between two trees.

The left aileron was torn completely off, along with two and a half feet of the left wing. The right wing, from the pitot tube outboard, was slashed back halfway through the wing section but did not break off.

The pilot started a gradual climb, circling to gain altitude in an attempt to bring the plane back to base. He then pulled the emergency canopy release and had to bump the canopy off, as he was still in a climb. The plane had to be steered by tail alone, but was operating satisfactorily. There was a burst from the right machine guns, probably due to a short in the wiring, so the pilot cut the gun switch and continued climbing.

Fire broke out in the gun section of the right wing and the ammunition started firing, so he figured it was time to depart. The pilot bailed out.

Many strange and some amusing things occurred during the Sicilian campaign. The pilots were always after locomotives when they could locate them. On one occasion the Italian engineer was most co-operative. The A-36s flew a course parallel to the train and the engineer sighted them and brought his train to an immediate halt. Waving to the pilots, he jumped from the cab and ran for cover. The fighter-bombers then proceeded to shoot up the train.

Many Sicilians assisted the pilots by pointing out camouflaged targets on the ground. The A-36s would come over low and the peasants would wave and point to German installations hidden in the trees.

Lieutenant Robert E. Fromm sighted a convoy of German light tanks on one of his missions. He opened fire and saw his tracers strike a tank and then he lined up on his second target, a truck.

"Thirty feet off the ground and nose slightly down, I sent six streams of lead into the truck. Instantly there was an explosion which enveloped him in flames and dark smoke. I had shot up an ammunition carrier.

"That was my first bad break. The second came a moment later when my plane, which was partially damaged by the blast, came out of the smoke at better than 400 miles per hour and plowed into a tree.

"I should say plowed *through* a tree. The plane continued to fly, but I knew it couldn't stay up for long. I climbed to 500 feet and I rose in my cockpit to bail out. But I looked down and saw Germans. I decided to stay with my ship for a while, as long as it would stay with me.''

The plane did stay with Fromm, although he could get it no faster than 160 m.p.h. nor higher than 900 feet.

With wings badly damaged, fuselage torn and dented, engine streaming smoke, his machine guns camouflaged by tree branches, he flew back toward friendly territory.

Fromm thought he had it made, but found himself over a flak area. ''I couldn't take evasive action, so I flew straight through it.''

He came down to land, thinking he had two wheels, but he had only one. ''I knew I landed on one wheel. So I lowered the left wing a bit. The field was slippery, and when the left wing hit the runway it skidded along instead of catching.'' Fromm stepped out uninjured.

A pleasant view of an A-36 showing armament to advantage: two .50 caliber guns in each wing (taped over to protect muzzles) and two in the fuselage, synchronized to fire through the prop arc. (USAF)

Lieutenant J. B. Walton of the 27th Group had this to say of a typical day's strafing, "We started after a convoy of 50 to 75 trucks. The captain went after the trucks ahead and I took those on the right. One truck started to turn back off the road and got caught in a gully and I got him just as he toppled over.

"Then I swung over to the side of the mountain we were passing. There were two trucks carrying about thirty men each. The men started running and I got both trucks. Then I went over a hill and got three more — all big trucks hauling men. Got them clean; I could see my tracers kicking up the dust around them. Then our flight ran into a locomotive and I saw it go up in steam. There was some ack-ack around this and I could see men standing around a gun. I was over to the right and they didn't see me. I shot all the men on the gun and damaged the gun."

Walton tells of another day when American aromored columns were trying to get around a narrow strip of sandy beach. "Each time one of our tanks would stick his nose around the bend, a hidden 88mm gun would open up. The tankers called for air support and the A-36s came in to see what we could do about the situation. The tank commander said he would risk one more tank, and for us to see if we could spot the culprit. Just as the tank showed itself, the Germans fired a round and we spotted the gun. It was on a mountainside inside a farm house. We then proceeded to remove the nuisance."

Lieutenant Wendell Hook of the 86th Group had always wondered if self-sealing tanks were as effective as the manufacturers claimed. He found out one day while was pulling off a target in string formation. A 20mm shell had gone through the left wing tank of the A-36 that he was trailing. For a few seconds, gas leaked out rapidly. Then it stopped. The pilot continued back to base some 100 miles away and landed. Hook had found out what he wanted to know.

Another A-36 pilot came in on a target over Italy, flying only 40 feet above the ground. He gave it a short burst at 300 yards and a violent explosion occurred. As he was almost over the target, he had to fly into the erupting debris. Exploding shells came through the floor of the cockpit, but luckily he was not wounded. The wings were full of holes and the ailerons were almost blown off. Large holes up to six inches in diameter were punched in the wings and the metal was peeled and jagged.

There were holes in every section of the wings, and the right wing tip was partly torn loose and pointing upward. The horizontal stabilizers were bent upward and full of holes and the leading edge of the left horizontal stabilizer was blown away. The rudder and elevators were still controllable. The cockpit filled with smoke, but the pilot noted that he had 1200 feet of altitude.

After flying some 20 miles, the engine started to quit, so the pilot bailed out. He was picked up shortly by an Italian speedboat and was made prisoner. A few days later he was turned over to the Americans when they captured the small island where he was being held.

On another mission several of the Invaders of the 27th Group were flying at minimum altitude. They were just above the whitecaps off the coast of Italy when the geysers of water began to kick up beneath them. At first the pilots paid little attention to them and one even stated that he thought they were porpoises playing. Then it was discovered that the planes were being fired upon by 88mm guns on the coast! Suddenly an 88mm burst sent up a column of water directly ahead of one of the A-36s. The pilot didn't have time to recover; his plane hit the water with a smack but stayed right side up. The pilot, uninjured, went over the side, got into his dinghy and paddled to shore. He, too, was liberated when Italy was invaded.

The A-36s didn't see much aerial combat, but their pilots had always been told that they were no match for the Me 109 at high altitude. If bounced by Germans, they were to salvo their bombs and force the fight to their altitude below 8000 feet; preferably below 5000.

These tactics paid off for three A-36 pilots who encountered opposition south of Rome in September 1943. The Americans, a flight of eight, had been making about 300 mph, shooting up ground targets and flying so close to the ground that they had to pull up to get over the trees when they spotted a flight of three Me-109s.

Lieutenant Eugene Santala related, ''The Me's were also low, but higher enough that they didn't see us, although they were only about a quarter of a mile away. We turned and chased them for five minutes, keeping low. Just as they banked to come into their field to land, they saw us. But it was too late then, for we already closed up.

''I picked up my target, having advantage since I was leading the flight. The Me seemed to fall apart. The wreckage fell practically on the field. Flying Officer James F. Roberts, who was flying my wing and had shot a short burst at a plane, slipped down to the air base and perforated an He-111 — it blew up.''

Lieutenant Robert Allen then cut off the second Me-109 and shot it down. The third German, in a desperate attempt to avoid the A-36s, cut away and headed for the nearby mountain with the Americans in hot pursuit. Five times the planes roared around the peak. Then the leading Invader lost his pole position among the A-36s when he skidded off course in the attempt to close for a shot. He tried to fly over the mountain and get at Jerry from an angle, but this failed, too. The second pilot hung close to the Messerschmitt's tail, managed to gain a little and finally filled his sights with the 109. A short burst was all that it took.

The most successful A-36 pilot, as far as enemy aircraft went, was Lieutenant Michael T. Russo. He had his biggest day on December 30, 1943, when he led

Lieutenant Michael T. Russo of the 522nd Fighter-Bomber Squadron was the first Mustang ace and the only pilot with five kills in the A-36. (Russo)

a twelve-plane formation to attack a railroad station near Rome. While flying at 14,000 feet approaching the target, sixteen Me 109s attacked the A-36s. Remembering his teachings, Russo immediately took his flight down to 8000 feet with the enemy in hot pursuit. At this altitude the A-36 could give the Messerschmitts trouble and this they did. Turning into the enemy, the Invaders broke up the formation and Russo accounted for two of the fighters before the dogfight ended. These victories raised his total to five, making Russo the first Mustang ace and the only A-36 ace.

The A-36, which had shown excellence in bombing, strafing and as a low-altitude fighter, demonstrated further variety when it was used as a supply craft. After Salerno, Lieutenant Walton and three other pilots flew food and ammunition to some stranded American paratroops. The packages were heavily wrapped and hung on the bomb racks of the Invaders to such an extent that they could hardly get off the ground. All the way to the drop zone the pilots had to fight to maintain control as the bulky packages tried to sway in the racks. Finally they made the drop zone and let the bundles go at zero altitude. The supplies were delivered in good shape.

Maintenance on the A-36s proved to be excellent. No great difficulties were experienced, and the majority of the aircraft were kept flyable. The ground crews of the 86th got a rare chance to appreciate the results of their good work when the group moved to Italy in mid-September of 1943.

The unit had just moved to Sele strip when they were called upon to destroy a large tobacco-factory building on the outskirts of Battipaglia. The factory buildings were serving as stronghold for a dozen 88mm guns and 150-plus Germans who were holding up the advance of the X Corps.

At one o'clock on the afternoon of September 17, the first squadron of the 86th took off and swung out over the bay to get altitude. Then they came back across the field and made a turn to the south along the main coast road. That brought them over the target. Down they went, raining their 500-pound bombs. At Sele strip the ground crews stood and watched the bombs, which they had loaded only 15 minutes previously, fall on the factory.

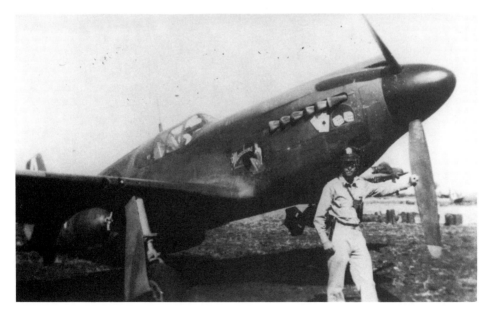

"Moraleene" was an Invader of the 27th Fighter-Bomber Group, flying with the Twelfth Air Force during the Italian campaign. (USAF Museum)

A second attack was made on the German stronghold late that afternoon and a third early the next morning. Shortly after the last raid the X Corps moved forward and took over. The 86th had blown the place to bits. Twelve guns and over a hundred Germans were found in the wreckage.

Forty years later, much is still written and spoken regarding the immortal P-51 Mustang, but little is remembered of her sister, the A-36. Yet the Invader did a tremendous job in those days of 1943 when so much hung in the balance. When our ground troops needed air support so badly, it was the A-36s that gave it to them. Surely those infantrymen have never forgotten this aircraft, nor have the surviving Germans who still recall the screaming demon of the Mediterranean.

CHAPTER 3

AAF MUSTANGS IN ENGLAND

In the late summer and early fall of 1943, the bombers of the Eighth Air Force had suffered heavy casualties at the hands of the Luftwaffe fighters. The primary cause of these losses was the inability of their escort to accompany them all the way to such targets as Schweinfurt and Regensburg, deep in Germany. The utilization of two 108-gallon drop tanks provided the P-47s with a theoretical range of only 375 miles and this didn't allow for aerial encounters. At that time Lockheed P-38s equipped two fighter groups in England, but their range wouldn't allow them to go all the way with the bombers, either. The operational planners wanted desperately to begin an all-out bombing campaign against the industries underlying the Luftwaffe, but with no long-range escort fighters, further deep penetration into Germany by Eighth Air Force bombers was out of the question.

A few early P-51As and F-6s had found their way into the tactical-reconnaissance units of the Eighth Air Force at this time, but the first of the Mustangs destined for fighter units had not arrived. Operational leaders in England were well aware of the extended range of the P-51, and were anxious to test it as bomber escort, even though the Mustang would not be able to go to all targets with the bombers until it was fitted with drop tanks. Regardless, the arrival of the new aircraft was eagerly awaited in the theater. However the first fighter unit to be equipped with the Mustang in England would be assigned not to the Eighth Air Force, but to the Ninth!

On November 4, 1943, a tired but eager group of young pilots was unceremoniously delivered to the airdrome at Greenham Common in England. New to the European Theater and with no combat experience, they were still awed with the whole situation and, other than rumor, had no idea they were to pioneer a new concept in fighter-escort tactics. They were the 354th Fighter Group, and it was their good fortune to have been selected to become the first P-51 Mustang fighter unit in England.

Jubilation was the order of the day for Lieutenant Colonel Kenneth R. Martin's pilots at Greenham Common when orders came for him to select a nucleus of pilots

A shiny new P-51B displays its classic silhouette — a form which became revered by heavy bomber crews during late 1943. (McDowell)

to train on the P-51As of the 67th Tactical Reconnaissance Group. After a few days of flying, these pilots returned to Boxted where their own Mustangs had begun to arrive. The newcomers immediately fell in love with the P-51, and the 354th adopted the name of the "Pioneer Mustang" Group.

The Eighth Air Force had watched the training and performance of the 354th with anxious eyes, and as the group neared its initial operation, it found itself still the property of the Ninth Air Force, but assigned to the Eighth for operations.

By December 1, 1943 the unit had received 54 P-51Bs and three P-51B-5s, and on this date 24 planes and pilots were dispatched on a familiarization sweep over the Knocke-St. Omer-Calais area. The mission was led by the famed CO of the 4th Fighter Group, Colonel Don Blakeslee, a former RCAF and Eagle Squadron pilot. The steely-eyed Blakeslee greatly impressed the new Mustang pilots in briefing that morning when he informed them that in a head-on attack from the enemy, his pilots didn't break. When a young pilot asked him, "What if the German doesn't break either?" his reply was, "Son you will have earned your hazardous duty pay."

The 354th encountered its first enemy aircraft on December 13 while escorting the bombers to Kiel. Lieutenant Glenn T. Eagleston and Lieutenant Wallace Emmer were in a two-plane formation when they observed an Me-110 about 3000 feet below them. Eagleston dived under Lieutenant Emmer and came in on the tail of the Messerschmitt. His first burst of gunfire seemed to have no effect, but on his second pass the P-51 pilot silenced the rear gunner.

The first USAAF Mustang group to fly from England was the 354th, which commenced operations in November 1943. "Peggy" belonged to the 355th FS.

"As I came in again I fired short bursts from 300 yards astern and from slightly above. I knocked out the 110's right engine which burst into flame, parts flying off the engine. I broke off at extremely close range. On my fourth pass I came in from astern and slightly above, but my guns were jammed and I broke off without firing," reported Eagleston.

The Me-110 was last observed in a shallow dive with the right engine out and aflame, heading down into the overcast. A Mustang pilot had made the first of many marks against the Luftwaffe, even if the claim did have to go in the records as a probable.

The first confirmed victory of an AAF Mustang pilot was gained by Lieutenant Charles F. Gumm of the 354th while escorting B-17s to Bremen on December 16. In his own words, "While climbing in mutual support position with Lieutenant Talbot toward the lead box of bombers, we sighted four Me-109s starting to queue up behind the second box of bombers. We climbed after them, and when in about 400-yards range, two enemy aircraft saw us and broke left and straight down. We closed on the other two and I dropped back a little to cover Lieutenant Talbot's tail, but his 109 saw him and broke left and down.

"I was then almost in position to fire on mine who was still flying straight for the bombers. Lieutenant Talbot pulled up and to the right to cover my tail while I closed to about 100 yards. I fired a two-second burst, noticing no effects. Closed to about 60 yards and fired a three-second burst, noticing a thin trail of smoke coming from the right side of the engine. I fired again at very close range and was showered with smoke, oil and pieces which I pulled up through, and glanced back to see him going down to the left with a large roll of smoke coming from the right side of the engine. Then I looked for Lieutenant Talbot again and saw him chasing a 109 and another 109 closing in on him. Went down after the last 109 and they broke straight down and we went back to the bombers.''

The Pioneer Mustangs had their first big day on January 5, 1944, when Major Jim Howard led them to Kiel to give the ''big friends'' target and withdrawal escort. In the area between Meldorf and Kiel, large concentrations of twin-engine fighters were encountered. Scores of Me-110s were lobbing their rockets into the bomber formations when the Mustangs tore into them and completely routed their attacks. When Jim Howard rounded up his P-51s to come home, eighteen of the enemy had been shot from the sky while Lieutenant Warren Emerson, who had been hit by 20mm fragments, was the only casualty of the 354th.

Six days later, Major Howard led the group again; this time to Halberstadt and Oschersleben. The fighters were assigned to provide target support for the bombers,

Lieutenant Colonel Jim Howard, originally CO of the 356th FS, became leader of the 354th ''Pioneer Mustangs.'' He was the only Eighth Air Force fighter pilot awarded the Medal of Honor, and was one of few earning the ace title in both the Pacific and Europe.

and upon rendezvous he positioned his Mustangs up and down over the bombers. In adherence with normal escort tactics, the P-51s broke up into flights of four and positioned themselves above and to the sides of their assigned bomber units. From this vantage point they enjoyed freedom of movement over the Fortresses, yet they held an altitude advantage over any German fighters that might rise to intercept the bombers.

The first enemy opposition was encountered as the bombers passed over the target. Mustangs dived down in an attempt to head them off, and in the melee, the eager pilots jumped the gun and cut in front of Major Howard, causing him to have to pull out of the attack. Alone, he headed for another bomber formation that was under attack and the events that then transpired are best related by Jim Howard. "When I regained bomber altitude, I discovered I was alone and in the vicinity of the forward boxes of bombers. There was one box of B-17s in particular that seemed to be under attack by six single- and twin-engined enemy fighters. There were about 20 bombers in a very compact formation and the fighters were working individually.

"The first plane I got was a two-engined German night fighter. I went down after him, gave him several squirts and watched him crash. He stood out very clearly, silhouetted against the snow that covered the ground. He went down in a cloud of black smoke and fire and hit the ground.

"Shortly after that, a Focke-Wulf came cruising along beneath me. He pulled up into the sun when he saw me. I gave him a squirt and I almost ran into his canopy when he threw it off to get out. He bailed out.

"Then I circled trying to join up with the other P-51s. I saw an Me-109 just underneath and a few hundred yards ahead of me. He saw me at the same time and chopped his throttle, hoping my speed would carry me ahead of him. It's an old trick. He started scissoring underneath me, but I chopped my throttle and started scissoring at the same time and then we went into a circle dogfight, and it was a matter of who could maneuver best and cut the shortest circle.

"I dumped 20-degree flaps and began cutting inside of him, so he quit and went into a dive with me after him. I got on his tail and got in some long-distance squirts from 300 or 400 yards. I got some strikes on him but didn't see him hit the ground.

"I pulled up again and saw an Me-109 and a P-51 running along together. The Mustang saw me coming in from behind and he peeled off while the Messerschmitt started a slow circle. I don't remember whether I shot at him or not. Things happen so fast it's hard to remember things in sequence when you get back."

However, the bomber crewmen remembered. On his return, the commander of the B-17 group immediately got on the telephone to Eighth Air Force Head-quarters to report the show that had been put on by a Mustang pilot who had taken on some thirty German fighters alone and had shot down six of them! Howard was identified by the code letters on his airplane and the military and the press descended upon him. Initially, all the information that they could get out of the modest Howard was, "I seen my duty and I done it."

Jim Howard's combat report doesn't mention the other enemy aircraft he fired upon which were seen to go down by the men of the B-17s, nor would he even claim more than three. Regardless of his reticence, his extraordinary feat and heroism were recognized with the award of the Congressional Medal of Honor.

Other Mustang pilots of the 354th downed another dozen German fighters that day for the loss of none of their own.

While victory was steadily increasing for the Mustangs, there had been hardship, too. Not only were pilots being lost to some of the better members of the Luftwaffe, but the P-51s ran into increasing difficulties from their fellow escort pilots. This stemmed from a recognition problem. The P-51 at a quick glance bore a close resemblance to the German Messerschmitt 109. More than once the Mustangs were attacked by P-47s, and there were occasions when they were damaged so badly that they barely managed to limp home. Lieutenant Glenn Eagleston, who was destined to become the top-scoring ace of the Ninth Air Force, was one of these victims. He was shot up so badly on one mission that he was forced to bail out over England. Some vehement letters from the 354th to Headquarters of the Eighth Fighter Command brought about some intensive aircraft recognition classes for the Thunderbolt pilots in England.

It wasn't all friendly opposition that was proving costly to the Mustangs, however, and at times the P-51 really had to show its stuff to get home to England. One of these early mission incidents is related by Lieutenant Clayton Gross.

"We had escorted a bomber group to Frankfurt on February 8, 1944, without a sign of the Luftwaffe, and reluctantly turned for home at the end of our tour without a man breaking the tapes on his guns. In the process of escorting the big friends we had separated into elements, and by chance when we started home, Lieutenant Radojits and I joined with an element let by Lieutenant Jim Daglish.

"After maybe thirty minutes we spotted a lone Messerschmitt 109 at about 2000 feet, silhouetted against a solid overcast. Naturally, Daglish and I had a race to get to him, but he popped into the overcast. We were quite disappointed and began to climb again; still watching the place for his exit. We were up a few thousand feet when he reappeared. Again we went down, but lost him again. As we began to climb again in mutual support, we still focused some attention on the cloud cover, although we had no intention of going down again. I casually glanced over to Daglish's element on my left and was astonished to see four FW-190s boring in on his tail.

"I screamed for them to break left so that Tony Radojits and I might fall in behind the attackers. Jim's wingman was hit severely as they began to break.

Captain Clayton K. Gross and his P-51B, "Live Bait." Gross learned that the Mustang could sustain heavy battle damage and still limp home. (Gross)

(He was downed.) I screamed again for Tony to follow me and broke hard left to get in behind the Focke-Wulfs as they went after Jim. When Tony didn't answer, I stole a quick glance over my shoulder and lo and behold, Tony was gone, and I had four Focke-Wulfs on my own tail and already firing at me. I recall that I wished Daglish the best of luck and continued my roll left to the inverted position, at which time I pulled back and headed for that friendly cloud cover at 2000 feet.

"I entered the undercast at some ungodly speed with no instrument uncaged and no idea of what lay below me. I can recall how great the landscape looked below when I pulled out without hitting anything. I had placed the throttle through the gate into "war emergency" (i.e., an extreme throttle setting which allowed absolute full-engine power. Normally, five minutes operation at this setting was enough to damage the engine.) As soon as I leveled off, because I expected the entire Luftwaffe to be behind me at any moment. I went to the deck — and I mean grass cutting — and immediately set sail for home.

"The first item which popped in front of me as I steered for England was a locomotive which required no movement on my part to hit as I approached. I remember my feeling as I passed over it. I knew I was going down and I thought, 'Oh, boy, that's going to make them mad.'

"A few minutes later I saw a truck on the highway at about my level, and since it had German markings, I proceeded to blast it, after which I again experienced some regrets thinking about the consequences as soon as they got me.

"I had several targets which I could not resist and I think the same thoughts entered my mind each time. I truthfully did not relax until I reached the English Channel, and then not very much. Incidentally, at one time from my 1½-foot level, I spotted heavy power lines in front of me and for some reason reefed back in an attempt to clear them. I didn't make it. There was a tremendous explosion as I flew through them, but it stayed in the air. When I landed, I discovered that the collision with the wires had cracked my windshield, torn the air scoop off leaving the radiator exposed, imbedded a 2½-foot length of copper cable in the radiator and had taken a part of the wing tip off.

"This incident plus the fact that as I circled to land I discovered that I was still in war emergency and had been for a period of 45 minutes or over, instead of the maximum five minutes, was nothing short of a miracle."

Neither Gross nor Daglish's wingmen returned from the mission. But Gross went on to become a six-victory ace flying the Mustang.

The P-51B with its 70-gallon fuselage and internal wing tanks could escort to a point approximately 475 miles from base, which was 100 miles better than the

A startling photo revealing an Me-410 after putting a cannon shell through the wing of a 388th BG B-17. This could lead to . . .

This. A 305th Fortress goes down shedding parts with number two afire. (USAF)

But long-range P-51s led to this: an Me-410 framed in a fighter's gun camera. Which in turn led to . . .

This: an unmolested formation of the 95th Bomb Group over Norway. P-51s with drop tanks could escort heavies almost anywhere. (USAF)

maximum escort range of the P-47 equipped with two 108-gallon wing tanks. Early in March of 1944 the Mustang demonstrated what it could do with two 75-gallon tanks, it illustrated its versatility by increasing escort range to 850 miles. The bombers then had an escort that could go anywhere they could go. The time had come to penetrate all the way into the very heart of the Third Reich; the target — Berlin!

Four P-51 groups were operational in England at this time: the "Pioneer Mustang" 354th; the 357th Group which entered combat with the Eighth Air Force on February 10, 1944; the 363rd Group of the Ninth Air Force which was also assigned to the Eighth for operations and through persistence, Colonel Don Blakeslee obtained the sleek Rolls-Royce-powered craft for his 4th Fighter Group of the Eighth Air Force on February 25, 1944.

The bombers and their escorts were briefed to strike the Berlin area on March 3, 1944, but the weather proved to be appalling. All aircraft were instructed to abort the mission, but the call didn't get through to all of them. Nine pilots of the 4th Fighter Group searching for their "big friends" between Berlin and Hamburg found themselves surrounded by some 60 to 80 enemy aircraft.

Led by Captain Don Gentile, the Mustang pilots dropped their tanks and turned into the attack. Two pair of FW-190s split-essed and immediately two P-51s raced after them. This was just what the Germans wanted, for immediately Luftwaffe fighters pounced on the pursuing P-51s and shot one of the Americans from the sky.

Desperately, Gentile fought his way out of the encircling trap and then blazed back into the melee to help out. Quickly he lined up an Me-110, only to have his canopy frost up. Reefing in tightly, he fired a burst at a twin-engined Dornier 217 and registered good strikes before his gunsight went out.

Breaking off combat, he went streaking to assist Lieutenant W. W. Millikan who was in difficulty. But at the same instant, Gentile came under successive head-on attacks from four, two and then eight 190s. Slamming his throttle to the fire wall, Don climbed sunward as his supercharger cut in. A 190 loomed ahead. He gave him a squirt using Kentucky windage to compensate for his inoperative gunsight. The Focke-Wulf flamed.

Lieutenant Vermont Garrison blasted one enemy aircraft, and then with only one gun firing, he picked off another with a deflection shot.

Lieutenant K. E. "Swede" Carlson and three others went after a number of Me-110s that had gone into a protective Lufbery circle. "Swede" decided his tail-on approach wasn't going to work so he reversed his tactics and went after them in the opposite direction. One of the Messerschmitts broke out to attack. Carlson fired and hit the Me-110's port engine and the German went down.

Eight Luftwaffe fighters had fallen to the Mustangs when the Debden-based boys tore away to make their run for home. However, the ordeal of the remaining P-51s wasn't over. Increasing bad weather and squalls forced them to the deck. The flak batteries were by this time fully alerted and multicolored balls of fire began to arc the sky.

As four of the P-51s raced over a town, fireworks erupted with a vengeance. Vermont Garrison took a hit, bade his mates farewell, jettisoned his canopy and bailed out. For the quiet ace from Kentucky, the war was over.

Lieutenant Millikan managed to limp into Manston with five gallons of fuel left. An utterly exhausted pilot pulled himself from the cockpit, shakily descended from the wing, dropped to his knees and pounded the ground. After six hours of strife, his Mustang had brought him home. Seven of the nine P-51s had made their way back.

Top aerial scores in the 4th Group were posted by Majors Don Gentile and Duane Beeson. They logged 16.50 and 5.33 kills respectively in the P-51, both having flown Spitfires and P-47s previously. Beeson was downed by flak on April 5, 1944 with a total 17.33 aerial victories and remained a POW until war's end. (USAF)

On March 4, the bombers went back to the Berlin area in spite of a continuation of foul weather. Leading the pack was Don Blakeslee and his red-nosed 4th Fighter Group. This day the pilots would taste blood once more, and better yet, they actually got to see Berlin through breaks in the clouds before encountering the enemy. However, Blakeslee knew utter frustration when he pulled in on the tail of an Me-109 and his guns refused to fire. Grimly, he pushed his throttle forward and pulled alongside the 109, whose pilot answered his signal of disgust with a cheery wave. Blakeslee's claim to fame that day had been that he was the first Mustang pilot over Berlin.

Herein lay one of the few difficulties experienced in the P-51B Mustang. Gun stoppages became annoying for a period of time until the cause was discovered and remedied. Due to the thin profile of the wing, the guns mounted there had been canted to the inboard rather than mounted upright. In the course of combat maneuvers, "g" forces tended to cause the ammunition belts to bind, causing jamming. Installation of ammo-booster motors rectified this situation in short order.

Another unit was to taste defeat at the hands of the Luftwaffe that morning. Forty-eight P-51s of the 363rd Fighter Group set out from Rivenhall airfield as target escort in the Hamburg area. Heavy clouds were encountered and the formation became scattered and wandered off course. Near the target, the flights of two squadrons were bounced by Me-109s of II/JG 1 who claimed to have destroyed 12 of the Mustangs for the loss on only one of their own. The 363rd, in combat only two weeks, lost 11 pilots. This tragic loss was the worst ever experienced by a P-51 group in the ETO..

On March 6, the whole Eighth Air Force went to Berlin and, seemingly, the entire Luftwaffe came up to do battle. The 354th Group encountered over 50 of the enemy just after rendezvous, but these didn't want to mix it up. In the Brandenberg area a number of twin-engined, rocket-laden craft were engaged, and then some 109s got into the act. The Pioneer Mustangs claimed nine that day for the loss on one P-51.

The 357th Group, which had only entered combat in February, had one of its best days. Twenty Luftwaffe aircraft fell before their guns for no losses. The 4th

The 363rd Fighter Group of the Ninth Air Force was one of the first three USAAF units in combat with the P-51B. This white-nosed bird belonged to the 382nd Squadron. The group was redesignated a tactical reconnaissance unit later in the war.

Group did almost as well in downing 17. Major Howard "Deacon" Hively had nailed one Me-109, and got some good strikes on another when the German nosed over and dived straight down. Hively tucked his plane right behind the Messerschmitt and followed him until the 109 hit the ground. Hively's admiration for his Mustang is appropriately expressed in his combat report:

"A Mustang can outturn, outclimb, outdive and outrun Messerschmitt 109s."

Lieutenant Johnny Godfrey put a 109 in the trees that day. After three head-on passes, the Mustang pilot maneuvered behing the Messerschmitt and chased him right down on the deck among the trees. Abruptly, Godfrey snapped the stick back into his gut, but the German didn't make it. One wing was sheared off by the trees and the balance went cart-wheeling through the foliage.

The 354th Group received unexpected good news from a German broadcast on Aptil 7. Their commander, Colonel Kenneth Martin, had been lost on a mission to Frankfurt on February 11 when he collided with a German fighter. His pilots had last seen him spinning earthwards after the collision.

The German announcer related, "I have just returned from a visit to a hospital where I went to see an old friend of mine, who is a fighter pilot. I found my friend sitting up in bed, all smiles. He told me that he had been ordered to attack when U.S. bombers were over this country. He was approaching the enemy when suddenly he saw an enemy fighter coming straight for him at a distance of about a mile. He was piloting an Me-109 and the enemy plane was a Mustang. He did not swerve from his course; both machines were blazing away with their guns as they approached one another. They met full blast head-on. The German pilot remembers unbuckling his strap, then he found himself in the air, pulled his rip cord and came to earth with no more than a broken arm.

"I went to see Colonel Martin, who was in bed. He had the plaster cast taken off his left lower arm that morning and was then exercising his fingers, which had grown stiff. His only other injury was a broken right leg, still in plaster."

Spring of 1944 saw the 352nd, 355th, 359th and 361st Fighter Groups of the Eighth Air Force exchange their P-47s for Mustangs. Also entering combat with the P-51 was the 339th Fighter Group which had just arrived in the theater. The versatile ponies had shown their hooves to the Luftwaffe and were now ranging all over Germany with the bombers. Desperately, the hard-pressed German pilots took to the skies, but the P-51s were always there and in ever-increasing numbers.

A little over a month after the 352nd Group traded its P-47s for blue-nosed Mustangs, one of its pilots became the first in the ETO to knock five enemy aircraft out of the air on one mission. The group as a whole had a terrific day on May 8, with 27 planes destroyed, which was outstanding enough to warrant a Presidential Unit Citation in their first big battle with the new airplanes.

Major Bob Stephens of the 354th Fighter Group flew a string of Mustangs named "Killer." This is his P-51B with a Malcolm Hood, probably in May 1944. (USAF)

The fighters had rendezvoused with the bombers just short of Brunswick when gaggles of 109s and 190s arrived on the scene. Over 100 were flying in groups of 15 to 20, and all noses were determinedly pointed at the bombers.

The Mustangs proceeded to break into elements and attack the enemy force. Lieutenant Carl Luksic picked out a batch of fighters and chased them down to 3000 feet, where he lost them. With only his wingman, Lieutenant R.G. O'Nan, he leveled out and heard O'Nan sing out over the R/T, "There's a 109 ahead."

Luksic couldn't spot him so he told O'Nan to take care of him. "During the chase, I saw six 190s coming in from my left headed for the bombers, so I immediately turned into the sextette.

"I fired very short bursts from about 300 yards on the nearest 190, the tail-end Charlie. I saw many strikes on the canopy and fuselage. The pilot stopped short, rolled his ship over and bailed out. A moment later I saw the pilot of the plane that Lieutenant O'Nan hit bail out, too.

"The leader of these 190s evidently saw what had happened. He whipped his formation around and one of them started shooting at me. It became a rat race, with all of us going around in circles. Somewhere in this merry-go-round I managed to get on the tail of one of them. I fired a couple of bursts — but I'm sure none of them went home. The German must have gotten scared, for the next thing I knew he went into a spin. I saw him crash and explode.

"I shopped around for a while, thinking I could find some more targets to shoot at. I saw a lone plane at a distance, which I couldn't quite make out. It might have been friendly, but I wasn't sure, so I went to investigate. When I was 25 yards back of it I realized it was a bandit. I fired once. Next thing I knew I was flying his wing, right beside him. My speed had brought me right up to him. He looked at me. I looked back. I must have scared the hell out of him, for the next thing I knew he jettisoned his canopy and bailed out.

"All this action had taken place below 3000 feet. As a matter of fact, the third combat wound up at 200 feet. So I went for altitude. As I climbed, Captain Davis and Lieutenant O'Nan joined me. The three of us started back for the bombers which were dropping their loads over Brunswick. We reached no more than 2000 feet when off to my left about twenty-five bandits in close formation going down through the clouds, appeared. The three of us immediately went in to attack, and followed them through the clouds. I found myself directly astern of a 190, which had a 109 right next to it. I evidently was unseen, as I got in a very successful burst at the 109, observing hits on the wings, fuselage and tail. The 109 caught fire and went straight into the ground.

"The 190 kept right on going as if nothing had happened to his wingman. He was a perfect duck to shoot at. I registered hits on his left wing, engine and canopy. The 190 went into a tight turn spiral and crashed."

The attrition of a two-front war and years of combat were taking a toll of German pilots. While many of these intercepting formations, or gaggles as the Allied fighter pilots chose to call them, were led by veteran pilots who could give any American pilot and his Mustang a real run for his money, the ranks were being filled by youngsters inadequately trained for combat. The long range of the Mustang created hostile skies over all the training fields of the Third Reich, and insured that fewer capable pilots would be coming up to meet them.

Regardless of their experience, it seemed that the Luftwaffe pilots just didn't want to believe the performance of the Mustang. Invariably they attempted to outclimb or outdive the P-51 as is exemplified in the combat of Lieutenant Joseph L. Lang of the 4th Fighter Group on May 24, 1944.

"Shortly after rendezvous we saw 20-plus Germans climbing 5000 to 6000 feet above us and at 12 o'clock to the bombers. We dropped tanks and climbed toward them. Some of them seeing us, split-essed away. Several 190s tried to come around behind us, but for some reason they broke away. I closed my section up astern to four Me-109s. I noticed another Mustang pull in front of one of the e/a (enemy aircraft). The P-51 was clobbered very badly and started losing altitude, smoking and burning. I closed on a 109 and fired. I missed and he broke down for the deck. At 35,000 feet, he started diving straight down. I fired and hit him in the starboard wing root and fuselage. I did this twice more. Most of the time he was rolling. At 18,000 feet, I noticed I had 650 to 675 on the clock. He started burning, then he shed his right wing.

"I leveled off at 2500 feet above some broken clouds and saw an FW 190 on the deck. I went down to attack. When I was 300 yards from him, I cleared my tail and saw six FW 190s at six o'clock to me. I broke into them and was again bounced by a gaggle of 25 FW 190s.

"As there were three gaggles of 20-plus 190s, I had a busy time with them. When I saw I couldn't keep turning, I pushed everything to the gate and started climbing. They queued up in back of me and took turns shooting. Some of them kept climbing to the side of me and would make head-on passes at me. I finally hit some clouds at 18,000 feet and lost them. About 15 to 20 FW 190s followed me to the clouds. I believe the Mustang will outclimb anything the German has."

Lieutenant Glenn Eagleston had one of the most unusual dogfights of his career when he dove his P-51 at 700 miles per hour in pursuit of a Focke-Wulf 190 which he finally destroyed.

"The Jerry thought I was another German at first," said "Eagle", "because he started rocking his wings. I was very friendly and rocked mine right back, moving in closer. Realizing his mistake, the Jerry turned into me as I gave him a burst. Then he rolled over and dived in an attempt to shake me.

"I salvoed my wing tanks and went down after him. He kept diving, but I knew I had the best ship and stayed right after him. He tried to pull out at 6000 feet, but his ship wouldn't take it and he spun into the ground.

"I pulled out at 8000 feet and glanced down at the airspeed indicator. I saw the needle quivering around the 700-mile-per-hour mark. And about that time, the wing tanks I dropped at 23,000 feet whizzed past, missing me by a mere foot or two."

The 4th Group set a new ETO record on April 8, 1944 with a rousing 31 victories scored for the loss of four Mustangs. The red-nosed P-51s thundered into Germany escorting the bombers to aircraft plants at Brunswick.

Blakeslee had just brought his unit to the rendezvous with the B-24 Liberators when he sighted the rising horde of enemy aircraft.

"Horseback to all Horseback aircraft. One hundred plus approaching bombers at 11 o'clock," he snapped.

The Mustangs dropped their tanks immediately and broke for the Germans, but not before the first wave of Luftwaffe fighters had dropped on the lead box of B-24s. Six of the lumbering bombers took fatal wounds from the onslaught. They seemed to lurch and stagger under the fire of their attackers, then fell from formation streaming smoke and flame. Soon little wiggling objects could be observed emitting from the Liberators during their descent, and small white canopies popped out above them. Parachutes, smoke and debris seemed to fill the wake of the dying behemoths plunging to their destruction.

Captain Don Gentile, Captain Louis Norley and Lieutenant Millikan picked out their targets and headed for them. Millikan got in a good deflection shot and sent his victim spinning to earth.

Norley caught a 190 2000 feet below him and chased it down to 3000 feet. The German did a tight climbing turn to the left, but Norley dumped 20 degrees of flap and turned inside him. As the Focke-Wulf rolled over and headed for the deck, Norley jumped right on top of him. Two short bursts and the German bailed out.

Norley pulled up and went after another 190 that was diving down below him. This one he chased for a mile or more before he pressed the gun button and saw the canopy of the 190 pop, followed by a somersaulting pilot.

The Mustang pilot then got in another turning match with a 190. He finally clamped on the enemy's tail, but overshot. Norley did a wingover and met the Focke-Wulf head-on. The 190 split-essed for the deck with the P-51 hot after him. The American blacked out in his pullout and recovered at 4000 feet, expecting to find the Jerry on his tail. But, alas, the 190 had flown into the ground and was splattered in smoldering ruins over the landscape. This gave Norley a triple for the day.

Other 4th Group pilots were meeting with equal success. Gentile knocked down three and Millikan got another before he tangled with a wily Luftwaffe veteran who fought him all through the skies over Brunswick. Tenaciously the two fighter pilots whirled round and round, each seeking an advantage. Finally the German spun out of a flaps-down turn. Before the pilot could recover, Millikan scored with a beautiful 90-degree deflection shot. The 109 burst into flames but the pilot managed to get out at about 800 feet. Just enough altitude for the chute to pop and save the German to fight another day.

And so it went as the P-51s took the war home to the Third Reich. The bombers now went to targets with a minimum of losses to German fighters. In the meantime, Allied forces gathered in the armed camp that was England, awaiting the moment that they would hit the beach on the Continent and take the war to the Germans on the ground. The far-reaching bomber stream with its escort of high-stepping Mustangs helped hasten that day.

CHAPTER 4

EIGHTH AND NINTH AF MUSTANGS

D-day and Beyond

All of England had been abuzz since late spring of 1944 in expectation of launching the mightiest invasion fleet the world had ever known. Alert after alert had been called at UK air bases and the anxiety had reached a fever pitch. Finally the orders came; all personnel were restricted to base and maintenance men worked around the clock to prepare aircraft for the big day. All available assistance was called in to assist in painting the broad black-and-white identity stripes on the wings and fuselages of each plane that would be flying over the beaches.

All through the night of June 5-6, the steady drone of engines filled the English skies as C-47s bearing paratroops and pulling gliders headed for Cherbourg Peninsula to deposit the vanguard of Allied troops on the Continent. Long before dawn, bombers rose to assemble in the murky skies before heading in to bomb enemy positions, and fighter-plane props began to turn shortly thereafter.

D-day was actually a great disappointment to the fighter pilots. For months they had anticipated the presence of hordes of Luftwaffe planes filling the arena to challenge the invasion. D-day would be the fighter pilot's dream; the enemy would be everywhere. Alas, such was not the case. Eighth Air Force Fighter Command flew 73 patrol and 34 fighter-bomber missions that day but the only aerial opposition encountered was in the French interior. The Luftwaffe was as scarce as hens' teeth over the beaches. Most of the Mustang pilots had to be satisfied with attacks

One of the classic Mustang photos shows three P-51 models of the yellow-nosed 361st Fighter Group. Colonel T. J. Christian, the group commander, flies "Lou IV," a P-51D-5, while his wingman has a new D-25 with the dorsal fin. The second section from the 375th Squadron comprises a D and a B. (USAF)

on ground targets of opportunity. Eighth Fighter Command claimed 26 enemy planes in the air while losing 26 to all causes.

Once the Allied troops were firmly entrenched on the beachheads, ground-support missions became more and more a part of the job of the Mustangs. Of course this didn't detract from their primary mission of escorting bombers, but with the arrival of new fighter units, more aircraft became available for bombing and strafing.

As the infantry and armor tried to break out of the beachhead peninsula, many P-51s were utilized to prevent German reinforcements from reaching the combat area. Trains, railyards, tanks and trucks became the primary targets of the many sorties that were flown in support of the ground forces during the period shortly after the invasion.

All of these targets presented their own peculiar problems for the Mustang pilots. Ample warning on the strafing of trains was given the pilots of the 352nd Fighter Group by their commander, Colonel Joe L. Mason in these words: "On trains you always have the factor of a flak car being present. They can be mean. It depends entirely on what kind of a train you encounter as to what and how you handle the problem. Troop trains are juicy but will always have one or two flak cars that must be taken care of. Tank cars burn very nicely. We started the idea of dropping

Every mission begins well before takeoff — in this case, loading the guns of a 362nd Squadron P-51D of the 357th Group. (Olmsted)

half-full wing tanks into the side of wooden freight cars and the setting of gas on fire.''

An unusual, yet highly successful, strafing mission along the lines of which Colonel Mason spoke was carried out by the 357th Fighter Group on June 16. Lieutenant Colonel Thomas L Hayes, Jr. led the unit, which had been ordered to locate and strafe two trains between Poitiers and Angouleme in southern France. However, there was no information as to their exact position, type or content. Another group was called and it was agreed that the 357th would arrive ten minutes before them, with each unit sweeping the area south.

Colonel Hayes found that the only auxiliary gas tanks available were 108-gallon capacity, so it was decided that the tanks would be filled and each pilot was instructed to fly only 30 minutes on each tank, which would leave them about two-thirds full. The tanks would then be used as fire bombs.

The 357th arrived a bit early and began dropping down to find a hole in the undercast over the area. To quote Colonel Hayes, ''The only break in this cloud was the area from Poitiers to Angouleme, so I proceeded to search for trains. At the marshaling yard of Poitiers, rail transportation was seen. My top cover squadron, the 363rd, heard the conversation over the R/T, and when I started to lead down through a haze condition, they became separated and thought I was going down to attack. I was now leading the 364th and 362nd squadrons at 9000 feet, covering the railroad and main roads. Nothing was observed except a marshaling yard at St. Pierre, 30 miles south of Poitiers, with three lines of goods cars and other stray cars totaling one hundred cars in all. About one mile north, a train of 30 goods cars was rather neatly camouflaged by being parked between a cut of trees on a sharp bend. We flew south of Angouleme and observed congested traffic also at Angouleme, but I returned to St. Pierre as it looked like it was safe from flak.

"Having two squadrons now seemed to work smoothly and not too congested. As I mentioned before, the 363rd Squadron was raising hell at Poitiers at this time. Flying north on the sun side I left the 362nd at 9000 feet as top cover. I made a diving turn, slipping through some cloud at 3000 feet, and ended up on the deck, approaching the yard from the west or 90 degrees to it. My flight of four was slightly staggered abreast and coming in at 400 miles per hour, all firing ahead. As each one reached the cars, he released his tanks which sprayed the gasoline around. The second flight, not far behind, fired into the bursted tanks, setting many of the cars on fire; and then in turn released their tanks as they passed over.

"My second section of eight Mustangs at this time splashed their tanks on the 30 cars one mile north. After setting them afire, the cars began to blow up. We all made one pass, strafing to increase damage and fire. Then we pulled up to cover the 362nd while they got in on the fun. This second squadron picked out sections of cars and buildings still not burning. There was no use in strafing any more as the fires spread quickly. Now that the Germans could see what was happening, two flak cars started to fire, one on each side of the middle train. One element gave him two gas tanks while his wingman set the mess afire."

During the period of D-day and shortly thereafter, the new P-51Ds began to arrive in the theater. These new Mustangs were an appreciable improvement over the P-51Bs, not only by incorporating the more powerful V-1650-7 engine, but also with the new bubble canopy. The old greenhouse canopy of the P-51B had been the primary objection of the pilots since initial delivery of the aircraft for combat operations. The limited visibility in the earlier model had been partially improved in the fitting of the Malcolm hood on a number of P-51Bs operating in England. The utilization of this English-manufactured canopy made a tremendous difference in the visibility of the pilot, and as a matter of fact, some of the men who flew Mustangs contend that even the P-51D with the bubble didn't give them the field of vision that they enjoyed with the Malcolm hood.

During this period the first veteran P-38 group, the 55th, gave up its twin-engined Lightnings for Mustangs. The transition was accomplished in good order, but the change from the torqueless P-38 to the P-51 did present its problems. However, the greatest difficulty experienced by the former Lightning pilots was unfamiliarity with fuselage tanks. With a full load, an unstable flight condition was created by

A look in the cockpit of a new D model, fresh in its olive-drab camouflage. Prominent is the lead-computing gunsight, combat-tested by the 357th Group. (Olmsted)

the tank located right behind the pilot. The near-tragic consequences of the 55th, in transition due to this problem, is described by Major Edward B. Giller.

"Our first combat mission as a squadron flying P-51s with full internal and external tanks was a bit of a mess. I will never forget one incident. On climbing out from the base in full-squadron formation at 800 feet, the squadron in front of us had just pulled up into the lower cloud deck at 1000 feet when out of the bottom of the cloud came a spinning P-51. By some miracle of fate he dropped his tanks, recovered at about fifty feet with a permanently bent fuselage and in a very weak radio voice announced that he was aborting. I will never know to this day how he made the recovery. Needless to say, this unnerved the squadron, but everybody took a deep breath and climbed on into the soup. We made it to 25,000 feet but still had too much fuel in the fuselage tank. For some reason, at this point, a tight 360-degree turn was instigated which caused at least five pilots to spin out. All of these dropped their tanks and recovered somewhere below."

After a bit of experience in the new single-engined fighters, such an occurrence became a thing of the past for the former P-38 pilots.

A week or so after D-day, the Germans began their attack on England with the introduction of the V-1, ramjet-propelled pilotless plane carrying a high-explosive warhead. Lieutenant William Y. Anderson of the 354th Fighter Group became one of the first Mustang pilots to shoot down a "buzz bomb" when he encountered a V-1 on June 17 en route to a dive-bombing mission. He clocked the speeding "bug" at 400 mph before he got in position behind it and pushed the gun button. The warhead exploded and Anderson was lucky to get away without damaging his plane. P-51 pilots destroyed a number of V-1s in a similar manner during the summer of 1944.

While Allied troops were fighting from hedgerow to hedgerow in the fields of Normandy, the bomber offensive against strategic target in Germany went on relentlessly. A highlight of bomber operations in the ETO began on the morning of June 21. The 4th Fighter Group, led by Don Blakeslee, and one squadron of the 352nd Fighter Group teamed up to escort 114 B-17s on the longest one-way trip thus far in the war. The P-51s took a lot of runway that morning, laden with drop tanks filled to the brim. They would need every drop of fuel they could carry aloft, for their destination was Russia.

The Flying Forts dropped their bombs on the target at Ruhland and, other than heavy flak, the mission met with no opposition until in the vicinity of Warsaw, Poland, where 10 to 15 Me-109s showed up to block the way. The P-51s engaged

"The Hun Hunter from Texas" was Captain Henry W. Brown, who recorded 14.20 aerial victories before becoming a prisoner in October 1944. He remained the top aerial shooter of the 355th Group. (Marshall)

them and they tucked their tails and fled, minus five of their number. After seven and a half hours flying time the 1600-mile journey came to an end. The Mustangs whipped around in steep banks and set down on the strip at Piryatin.

That night there was a great celebration; feasting and drinking of fiery vodka toasts with the Russians. However, unknown to them, a Heinkel bomber had followed the American formation, and the Luftwaffe would be out with a vengeance the following night. For the first time American P-51 pilots knew complete frustration as they came under heavy bombing attack. Several of the Mustangs were destroyed, but they were lucky. At Poltava, the B-17s suffered appalling losses. Forty-four Flying Fortresses were destroyed on the ground.

The depleted force left Russia on June 26, with the bombers depositing their loads on Drohobycy, Poland, en route to AAF bases in Italy. After an uneventful mission the P-51s landed at Lucrera, in the land of the Fifteenth Air Force. The Eighth Air Force Mustangs were to see action when they joined the P-51s of the Fifteenth in escorting bombers to Budapest on July 2. The Luftwaffe rose to challenge and the 4th Group found itself in one heck of a dogfight. The outstanding performance of the day was turned in by Major H. D. "Deacon" Hively who

The opposition's most widely-employed fighter was the Me-109G, which lacked the P-51B's speed, turn rate and dive acceleration. But the Messerschmitt matched the Mustang in zoom climb and rate of roll. (Young)

The FW-190A was an even match for the 51 in most regimes but lacked the top speed and dive of the sleek Mustang. (Ambrose)

shot down one 109 and then was hit in the canopy by another 109. Despite glass in one eye and bloodied vision, he fought back like a tiger to blast two more of the 109s and then make his way back to Italy. A few days later, the fighter and bombers of the Eighth left Italy, flew an uneventful mission over France and returned to their respective English bases.

As Allied troops advance into France, construction was begun immediately on advanced landing strips for their fighter support. One of the first units to move to the Continent was the Pioneer Mustang 354th Group. Upon their arrival in late June the unit wasted no time in beginning operations. In view of their close proximity to the lines, it was no problem for their Mustangs to fly six and eight missions a day.

On the afternoon of July 23, Lieutenant John S. Miller of the 354th was flying a sweep over the combat area when his Mustang was hit by flak. He stayed with the aircraft as long as possible, but it soon became evident that he would have to bail out. After leaving the cockpit he regained consciousness to find himself hung on the horizontal stabilizer, the leading edge lodged in his belly. With both hands he flipped the leading edge over his head, fell clear of the P-51 and reached for the rip cord. It wasn't there, and he spent anxious seconds locating it around

Lieutenant Colonel Glenn T. Eagleston, another of the "Pioneer Mustangs," led the Ninth Air Force scoring column. At war's end he was credited with 18.5 shootdowns, pacing the 354th's Group's 38 aces.

on his back, where it had slipped. Once found, he popped the chute and landed without great injury to himself.

The Mustangs of the Eighth Air Force, too, continued to give excellent cover to the Allied armored columns that were racing across France. Major John L. Elder of the 357th Fighter Group was shooting up a fortified town ahead of the advance when his P-51 was hit by flak. He swung away and over a hill, getting right down on the deck. Then a pair of flak towers opened up on him, scoring new hits on his plane. Seeing flashes all around, Elder flew over another hill but not before the enemy had put a hole in his cockpit canopy and knocked out his radio.

Flying at more than 300 mph, he suddenly realized that he was heading directly at a string of high-tension cables, but it was too late to pull up. Plowing right on through, Elder saw sparks and smoke fly all over the place as one of the cables swapped around his vertical stabilizer and rudder. The P-51 was hard to control, but it still hung together. Knowing he would have to bail out, Elder decided to try to get a little altitude, only to find himself over German airfield which began pumping more flak at him.

Collapsed landing gear didn't prevent the 357th Group's Captain John Kirla from running up 11.5 aerial victories. He flew with the 362nd Squadron (Olmsted)

By now, the Mustang was really heating up and Elder jettisoned his canopy and flew out over the French coast. He tried to get near Cherbourg to cut toward land where he could set his plane down on the beach, but everywhere he looked he saw flak. Shaking his head, he headed the Mustang back over the English Channel where he accomplished a successful ditching. He was picked up by Air-Sea Rescue and was returned to England none the worse for his dunking.

One of the sterling triumphs that the Mustangs helped accomplish in the weeks following D-day was complete air superiority over the Allied area. Very few American or British troops were even bombed or strafed by the Luftwaffe. Not only were the German attacks broken up in the air, but the enemy airfields were hit repeatedly.

When VIII Fighter Command first permitted the P-51 pilots to go down and strafe on return from their escort missions in the spring of 1944, it had been possible to surprise German airdromes, shoot up a few planes and get away scot free. After D-day, Luftwaffe airfields became virtual armed fortresses bristling with flak towers, multiple light batteries stationed around the area and men on alert to man them at all times. These targets took a great toll of American pilots during World War II and cost many more fighter aces than the Luftwaffe ever shot down.

These missions had to be carefully planned and expertly executed to keep casualties to a minimum. To attain this objective, Colonel Don Blakeslee of the

4th Group had his own rules for airdrome strafing. They boiled down to three basic factors: surprise, speed and variation of the attack.

"I consider surprise as one of the chief factors in a successful strafe," said Blakeslee. "When my group is assigned to strafe a particular target, I ask for all photographs available. I want to know what the airfield looks like before I get there. I want my intelligence officer to get the best information he can on defenses, and I want to know what kind and how many aircraft are reported to be on the field and where I can expect to find them parked. I also want to know what the terrain around the airdrome is.

"With this I can plan the approach best calculated to achieve surprise. I use terrain for cover and airdrome installations to screen my approach; I never come right in on an airdrome if I can help it. If I have planned to attack an airdrome beforehand, I pick an initial point some ten miles away. I have my course from there to the drome worked out. Once in the air, I take my boys right past the airdrome as if I had no intention of attacking at all. At my initial point I let down and wing back flat on the deck. Once I hit the drome, I really get down on the deck. I don't mean five feet up; I mean so low the grass is brushing the bottom of the scoop."

However, even the best of plans could not succeed without casualties. An example was Major Don Beerbower, the leading ace of the 354th Group when he set out from the French airstrip on the afternoon of August 9. After making a pass on an airdrome about three miles north of Reims, drawing intense flak and seeing about 30 Ju-88s parked in revetments, Beerbower directed an attack. He went in on the field from east to west as a diversion to draw fire, while the other flights went in from north to south to hit the enemy aircraft. Completely disregarding himself, Beerbower faced the concentrated flak in a diving attack, destroying a Ju-88 and knocking out two gun emplacements while drawing the ground fire to his Mustang. Though successful in diverting the fire from his other pilots, Beerbower's plane was hit again and again. He pulled up, jettisoned the canopy and attempted to bail out, but he was too low. The chute popped but never blossomed.

As Allied spearheads thrust forward in the direction of Paris, the 354th Group, along with the P-47 and P-38 units of the Ninth Air Force, continued to sweep the ground and the skies in front of them. On August 16 the Mustangs were on a fighter sweep over the German lines in the vicinity of Dreux, France, when the air controller reported that 20 Me-109s had been sighted. The P-51s immediately sped to intercept. As they moved to engage, another 60 German planes dropped out of the overcast some 3000 feet above them.

"I lived a lifetime in those few minutes," says Lieutenant Ken Dahlberg. "I clobbered one and he went straight into the ground burning. Everywhere you looked,

Lieutenant Ken Dahlberg, yet another 354th Group ace who scored nine of his 14 kills in Mustangs. Downed by German fighters, he bagged three of them first and survived to return to combat. (Dahlberg)

there was a Mustang mixing it with three or four Jerries. I chandelled up into the midst of a gaggle of 109s. I picked one and tapped him. He blew up, showering my plane with oil and debris. My visibility was almost nil due to oil on my windshield, but I managed to make out a lone 109 and headed for him. Just then I noticed my oil pressure was down. Someone must have gotten on my tail and shot at me, but in the excitement I never knew it until then. My gunsight was also out, but by watching the tracer bullets I was able to spray the 109. He blew up. Four other 109s hopped my tail at the same time and I knew I had to bail out. I headed for the clouds so that Jerry wouldn't clobber me as I got out.''

Once in the clouds, Ken went over the side. As quickly as he left his plane, the din of combat disappeared, and as his parachute opened, silence prevailed. Slowly he descended to land on the estate of a prominent Franch family — Dennis and Madeleine Baudoin.

Landing almost at the feet of Madame Baudoin, he had hardly spilled his parachute when she rushed up to him. ''Run and hide immediately,'' she told him. ''This whole place is crawling with Germans.''

Moving as swiftly as he could, he headed into the trees and brush, making his way to a stream. Quickly, he waded into the water and submerged his body until just his face was above the surface. Guttural words and sounds came to his ears as German troops began to scour the grounds for the flier who had parachuted only a few minutes before. Resorting to a trick that many an American boy learned from Indian lore, Dahlberg broke off a reed, put it in his mouth and ducked his head under water. Here he remained for what seemed an eternity while the search continued.

Dahlberg finally ventured to raise his head, but stuck close to the bank of the stream and made himself as inconspicuous as possible until night fell. Then he heard a low voice calling, and cautiously he crept from the water and moved to answer. It was Dennis Baudoin, the owner of the estate, who had brought him food. After hastily downing a belated meal, he was shown to a small tentlike structure made of twigs and sticks that was to be his hiding place during his stay.

Dahlberg was kept in hiding for several days, but with the news that American troops were nearing Paris, the young pilot implored Dennis Baudoin to help him go out to meet them. The two dressed in civilian attire and set out to find the Americans. In the confusion of retreating Germans, they went unchallenged. After a day of bicycling, a jubilant Dahlberg and his French companion came upon advancing U.S. troops.

Another Mustang pilot was downed over occupied France on August 18, but his rescue was accomplished in quite a different manner than that of Dahlberg.

"My plane has been hit by flak. I'm gonna belly it in," reported Captain Bert Marshall, Jr. of the 355th Group.

Lieutenant Royce Priest, flying the number three position, pressed his R/T button, "Land in a road, coach," he said. "I'll land and pick you up."

There were shouts over the R/T, protests and avowals, instructions and counterinstructions, but in the end Priest had his way. He soon realized that the field in which Marshall had landed was too soft to permit a landing which would enable him to take off again. But there was another field about three quarters of a mile away where some Frenchmen were loading hay onto a truck. The field was practically cleared of grain, and only short stubble remained.

Cutting his throttle almost to stalling speed, Priest landed in the stubble and braked to a halt. To make a runway, he whirled the plane around and rolled back to the eastern end of the field where he had first touched down. Meanwhile, Marshall was running through plowed fields toward the plane. "It was tough going," he said, "I wasn't in shape for that stuff. I got pooped out. Every now and then I had to slow down to a fast walk. And I was kind of mad because I remembered I only had two American cigarettes and I didn't like the idea of sticking around in France with only two American cigarettes."

Priest turned the Mustang to the east once more, taxied out of the field, across the narrow road and into another hay field from which none of the stacks had

Lieutenant Royce "Deacon" Priest sits on the lap of Captain Bert Marshall, illustrating the manner in which they returned from France following Priest's daring rescue in August 1944. (Marshall)

been cleared. Marshall trotted up beside the plane. At that time conversation transpired in which, as Priest recalls, "There was a reasonable amount of profanity involved."

Finally Priest stood up in the cockpit, hurled his parachute to the ground and said, "Get in!" Marshall shook his head disparagingly and hopped up and got into the seat.

Seated in Marshall's lap, Priest gave the plane the throttle and taxied across the road to line himself up with his improvised runway. As the P-51 moved forward, the canopy slid back and struck Priest across the head. Marshall reached up with both hands and held it closed. At the end of the runway, Priest spied a large haystack and hauled the stick back to his stomach. They cleared the haystack by six inches.

The ride home was not the most comfortable the two ever had, but it was probably the happiest. The most surprised man was the tower operator when Priest called in to report his Mustang coming in for landing with two men aboard.

At least one other rescue of this type aboard a P-51 is recorded before several unsuccessful attempts were made. In view of the latter, orders were issued forbidding any further attempts of this nature.

White spinner and red cowl band identify WR-N as a 354th Squadron aircraft, one of the "Steeple Morden Strafers" of the 355th Group. (Marshall)

Rapidly advancing armored columns and infantrymen had carried the war to the German frontier by the fall of 1944. Allied air power had increased to the point where 1000-plane raids on the Third Reich had become the ordinary rather than the exception. Practically all major targets were now in Germany, and the Luftwaffe had drawn in the majority of its forces to defend the cities of the fatherland. Great numbers of enemy aircraft came up on occasion to do battle with the American planes, and the Mustang pilots continued to take their toll.

It was on such a day that Lieutenant William R. Beyer of the 361st Fighter Group got five, using his new K-14 gunsight. The Mustangs were escorting the bombers to Kassel on September 27, 1944, when some forty of the enemy were sighted as they broke through the bombers and headed for the deck. Beyer picked out a group of about eight FW 190s and attacked them from above. Quickly he lined up one and opened fire, closing from 400 to 100 yards. Good strikes were registered and the German pilot popped his canopy and spiraled off into a cloud. Beyer reefed into a tight 360 and went down through the cloud to finish him off. Just as he broke through, he spotted a parachute off to his right. One down!

Picking up his wingman, Beyer spotted another 190 who did his best to get away by doing split-esses and tight turns, but the P-51 hung right with him. Then the German made the fatal mistake of attempting to climb. Beyer let fly, hit him and the pilot bailed out.

"Ferocious Frankie" was flown by 361st Group ace Wallace E. Hopkins. All his P-51s were named for his wife, this B model being photographed at Bottisham shortly after D-Day. (USAF)

The Mustang pilot then pulled up and got on another 190 who absorbed one burst, called it quits, and went over the side.

Number four apparently had more experience, for he led Beyer a merry chase for a few minutes and finally chopped his throttle and dropped his flaps in an attempt to get the American to overshoot. Beyer did likewise and fishtailed to keep from overshooting. The pilot of the 190 went into a gentle turn as the slugs from the P-51 began to rip into him. The pilot bailed out while still under fire.

The fifth 190 pulled up in a steep turn and then broke for the deck. Desperately, he attempted to lose the Mustang on his tail and even tried to lead Beyer into some power lines. Beyer got up and over while the German went under the wires. The P-51 was then right on top of him. Beyer opened up at only 75 yards and the 190 plowed into the ground and exploded.

Still the German planes continued to rise, even though these inexperienced pilots often seemed to blindly follow the leader and to make colossal blunders. The gaggle of 190s that Captain Bill Whisner encountered southwest of Merseburg on November 21 didn't even bother to drop their tanks.

"Colonel J. C. Meyer told me to take a straggler who was on the starboard and rear of the formation of 190s," related Whisner. "as I closed on him, the formation turned about 45 degrees right and this straggler joined the formation. I fired a short burst at this 190 at about 400 yards, using the K-14, but observed no strikes. I closed to 200 yards, fired another burst, which covered him with strikes. Large pieces flew off and he fell into a spin, smoking and burning.

"I closed on another 190 and hit him with a good burst from about 150 yards, knocking pieces off. He fell off to the right and I hit him again at 15 to 20 degrees deflection from 100 yards or less. Again pieces came off and he fell into a flat spin. I watched this one go through a haze layer, still spinning and smoking. About this time the enemy seemed to be worried. I saw two of them break off and dive down, taking violent evasive action. I did not attempt to follow them, but stayed behind the formation.

"I closed up behind a three-ship flight which was flying almost line abreast, about 50 yards apart. I put my sight on the leader but before I opened fire, he broke down. I was then almost between the other two. I banked steeply to the right, then back to the left and hit the one on the right at less than 100 yards. Pieces flew off him and he fell off into a flat spin, smoking and burning.

"I was depending on my wingman, Lieutenant Waldron, to get the one on the left and he didn't fail me. I saw him hit the 190 which went down out of control, smoking.

"I closed on another 190 which was turning from left to right. He saw me and turned steeply to the right. I cut him off and hit him all over in a deflection shot of 15-20 degrees at 200 yards or less. He went in a vertical dive, puffing smoke and flame, and disappeared into the haze. At this time I saw another 190 going down. My wingman had gotten this one.

"I made a 180-degree turn right while watching him, and lost my wingman. The main formation of 190s was still intact, but only two planes remained in the other section. I firewalled everything and caught up surprisingly fast. I picked the last one, fired at him from 300 yards. Being slightly below, and due to the heavy contrails, I did not see any strikes on him. He snapped into a tight spin and went below me. I claim a probable on this one.

"I was very close to the main formation at this time. I picked out one of them and started firing from about 200 yards. He was completely covered with strikes and fell off into a dive. I turned and watched him and he broke into several pieces. I think his belly tank exploded. Up to this time, none of the 190s had dropped their belly tanks. I had plenty of time to plan my attacks and those tanks made the 190s extremely vulnerable. As I fired on this last one, the main formation dropped their tanks and dived down and to the left. I followed, but lost them in the haze. As I pulled up, I saw three of the 190s behind me, so I stood my plane on its tail and lost them.

"At about 23,000 feet I saw a 190 on a P-51's tail. I attacked him and fired a deflection shot from 100 yards. As I mushed past his line of flight, he flew through my fire. He then leveled out and I hit him from slightly above at 50 yards. My fire hit him in the cockpit and engine. His canopy flew off along with other large pieces. He went straight down with his engine burning and smoking. I joined Colonel Meyer and came out with them."

For his claim of six destroyed and one probable, Whisner was awarded five destroyed and two probables.

Multiple claims were frequent during the fall and winter days of the gaggles. In addition to the two combats just described, several other Mustang pilots scored five victories on one mission during this period. They were Captain C. E. "Chuck" Yeager of the 357th Group on October 22; Captain Donald S. Bryan of the 352nd Group on November 2; Lieutenant Claude J. Crenshaw of the 359th Group on November 21; Captain L. K. "Kit" Carson of the 357th Group on November 27; Lieutenant J. S. Daniel of the 339th Group on November 26 and Captain William J. Hovde of the 355th Group on December 2.

On the ground, German resistance became tenacious once the fatherland was invaded. Allied troops, who had raced through France, encountered very stiff

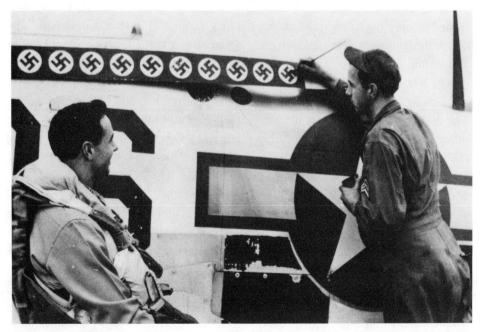

Major Fred Haviland of the 355th Group watches crew chief Gale Torrey notch up the tenth kill. Haviland finished the war with six air and 14 ground claims. (Marshall)

opposition at the Siegfried Line. Hopes for an end to the war in Europe in 1944 were dashed, and with the advent of winter, the lines became static.

Under cover of unseasonably bad weather, the Germans assembled their forces for a final, desperate offensive against the Allied forces. In the early morning of December 16, 1944, German panzer divisions, strongly supported by infantry, struck along a line between Monschau and Krewinkel, Germany. Swiftly, the onrushing German armor rolled into Luxembourg and Belgium. The Allies fought a retreating action to delay the enemy until reinforcements could be rushed forward to plug the gap.

The weather all but forced the Allied air forces from the skies, and missions in support of the beleaguered troops were kept to a minimum. However, Allied fighter units were rushed to advanced bases on the Continent. Among these were the 352nd and 361st Fighter Groups of the Eighth Air Force, whose Mustangs arrived in Belgium on December 23.

These units went into action immediately, as Eighth and Ninth Air Force fighters and bombers utilized the first break in the weather to hammer the German ground forces unmercifully.

It was on a support mission, while flying from the 352nd's advanced base at Asch, Belgium, that Major George Preddy, holder of the ETO record of six victories in one mission on August 6, 1944, met a tragic fate on Christmas Day. While

A rare formation shot of 364th Group P-51Ds. The 383rd Squadron's distinctive markings were holdovers from the group's P-38 days. (Field)

"Six down and no holes in me" is announced by Major George Preddy of the 352nd Group after the big scrap over Hamburg on August 6, 1944. Though tragically killed by US Army gunners on Christmas Day, Preddy remained the top-scoring Mustang ace. (USAF)

on patrol, enemy aircraft were reported in the vicinity of Coblenz. Preddy led his squadron to the position, spotted the enemy and turned into the attack. The Mustang pilot had just begun to gain an advantage in a turning match when another Me-109 cut in front of him. A short burst from Preddy's guns found its mark and the pilot bailed out.

Preddy turned back to his original opponent and latched on again. Once on the tail of the 109, a long burst produced numerous hits and again the pilot bailed out.

Preddy then received a new report of bandits in the area and this time he and two other P-51s headed for Liege, Belgium. As they approached, an FW-190 was spotted at about 1500 feet. The Focke-Wulf broke for the deck with the Carolina ace right on its tail. As he closed the distance to get in firing range, American antiaircraft opened up. The German fighter raced through the barrage, but as Preddy attempted to break off, he was hit repeatedly. The Mustang went up in a sharp chandelle, staggered and fell to the ground. The top-scoring Mustang ace of the ETO had fallen to friendly fire.

Through the use of airpower, the dogged resistance of the Allied troops was further enhanced to the point of stopping the German offensive in its tracks. The infamous "Battle of the Bulge" was over. By the end of December the full brunt of the German attack had been defeated.

The 352nd Group continued to operate from Asch throughout the German offensive, and was in a position to intercept on January 1, 1945, when the Luftwaffe made an all-out strike on Allied air bases in Belgium and Holland. Over 700 German fighters came in, skimming the ground, and wrought great destruction to many of the bases. The one bright spot for the Americans that day was the effort of the 487th Fighter Squadron of Mustangs. With Lieutenant Colonel John C. Meyer leading, 12 P-51s took off into the face of a strafing attack by 50 Me-109s and FW-190s.

One of the primary pilots involved in the air battle was Captain Bill Whisner. "After shooting down that first 190, I felt myself being hit," he said, "I had several 20mm holes in each wing and another hit in the oil tank. My left aileron control was also out and I was losing oil, but my pressure and temperature were steady. Being over friendly territory, I could see no reason for landing immediately, so I turned toward a big dogfight and shortly had another 190 in my sights. It went down with the pilot in it. The plane exploded and burned when it hit the ground.

"There were several 109s in the vicinity, so I engaged one of them. We fought for five or ten minutes and I finally managed to get behind the German. I hit the plane good and saw the pilot bail out from 200 feet. His plane landed in the vicinity of 15 or 20 others which had already been blasted out of the sky. My last victim, another 109, was trying to strafe an American airstrip. I landed strikes in the nose and wings of the 109 and saw it crash east of the strip.

"I chased several more of the enemy, but they got away in the clouds. By then I could hardly see as my windshield and canopy were covered with oil."

When things settled down over the base, Whisner came in for a safe landing.

Lieutenant Colonel John C. Meyer and his 11 pilots of the 487th tallied 23 victories that morning. Leading the scoring were Whisner and Captain Sanford K. Moats with four each. Captain Raymond H. Littge and Meyer each got two. This feat was accomplished without the loss of a single Mustang pilot. For their victory, the 487th was awarded the Distinguished Unit Citation, the only fighter squadron in the ETO to be so honored.

The Luftwaffe left 30 AAF and 120 RAF planes destroyed on the ground that day, but the price that they paid is indicative of their failure. Over 200 German fighters fell to the air and ground defenses.

By the spring of 1945, Nazi Germany lay in ruins. Allied ground forces pushed forward into Germany and seized the industrial Ruhr Valley. Tanks and infantrymen steadily fought their way toward the Rhine River and Berlin. Allied airpower so dominated the skies that their formations were overhead at all hours. Appearance

This unusual formation shot of 353rd Group aircraft demonstrates the effect of olive-drab paint on the upper surfaces. (Tanner)

of the Luftwaffe was sporadic and other than the jet threat, which is the subject of the next chapter, presented no great challenge.

It was not unusual for American fighters to sight bombers and cargo aircraft making mad dashes from one beleaguered airfield to another, so disrupted were the German communications and transportation systems. Many German military staff members and military dispatch couriers were forced to make use of the air rather than chance the highways which were constantly being strafed. Bomber types which American fighter pilots had never seen took to the air in these missions, as well as to make hit-and-run attacks on rapidly advancing Allied armored columns.

Captain C. B. East and Lieutenant Lee Larson of the 15th Tactical Reconnaissance Squadron were on an armed reconnaissance mission in the vicinity of Wittenberg when they sighted a Junkers 88 bomber. Captain East made the first pass, firing from 500 to 100 yards, scoring hits on the fuselage and setting the left engine on fire. Larson attacked from the other side and when he broke off, the right engine was burning. The big twin-engined craft went into a gentle glide. One man bailed out before the Junkers exploded.

An hour later, the two pilots sighted an FW-190 flying west at 2000 feet and opened fire from 100 yards. The Focke-Wulf crashed and burned. These encounters had no effect over the primary mission of the Mustang pilots. Captain East returned to file a thorough report on all marshaling yards and rail lines on his route.

Strategic-bombing missions continued relentlessly until the very end of the war in Europe. As long as the Fortresses and Liberators struck at the heart of Germany, the P-51s continued to escort them.

Lieutenant Colonel Sid Woods was leading the 4th Fighter Group in the vicinity of Berlin on March 22, 1945, when he sighted four bombed-up FW-190s heading for the Russian lines. Immediately he closed on the fourth man in the flight, gave him a burst and observed him nose over and hit the deck.

Woods then found himself under attack from another 190 coming in from his left at 90 degrees. He shoved the stick down and let him pass over. The P-51 pilot then pulled straight up, rolled off the top and came down on his tail. The 190 went into an aileron roll, with the P-51 firing away. With both aircraft on their backs, the 190 took hits and nosed down to crash on Furstenwalde airdrome.

Woods then caught another flight of four turning between Eggersdorf and Furstenwalde airdromes. He tapped the number four man with a two-second burst. The German immediately salvoed his bombs, jettisoned the canopy and went over the side.

Then the Mustang pilot sighted two 190s on the tail of a P-51 and dived down to hit one flying right above the ground. The German went in.

Climbing to 3000 feet, the 4th Group commander sighted another flight of four. Again he chose to close on number four, but as he came in on his tail, all of the

. . . and the smile on the face of the tiger. Lt. Col. Sid Woods of the 4th Group celebrates at Debden after bagging five FW-190s on 22 March 1945. His wingman, Lt. R. E. Moore, looks on. (Woods)

Focke-Wulfs broke violently to the left. Woods racked in so tight that his gyro spilled, so he had to give delfection with his fixed sight. As the German pulled into a steep climbing turn, the tracers caught him and strikes could be seen all over the cockpit. The FW caught fire, crashed and burned. This 20-minute fracas boosted Sid Woods' wartime total from two to seven.

The Mustangs of the Ninth Air Force's 354th Group were operating from a strip in northern France in the spring of 1945. Their proximity to the fighting front enabled them to fly many types of tactical missions as well as to escort bombers when the occasion arose.

Lieutenant Andrew J. Ritchey, with Lieutenant C. W. Salter flying his wing, was dispatched on a weather reconnaissance mission on April 2. The two Pioneer Mustang pilots sighted two FW-190s over Erfurt airdrome, preparing to land. Both P-51s dived down, firing. Both of the 190s crashed onto the airfield.

Ritchey and Salter then sallied forth over Gotha airdrome where they shot down a FW-190 which was flying at 3000 feet. Immediately after this encounter they saw 90-plus FW-190s and Me-109s in waves of eight, flying west at 3000 feet. Most of them were carrying belly tanks, apparently intent on destroying some of

A FW-190 takes hits in the right wing during violent maneuvering. (Rust)

the equipment being rushed to advancing Allied forces. The two Mustangs bounced the first two formations, claiming one FW-190 destroyed, one damaged and one Me-109 destroyed. Low on fuel and ammunition, the Americans headed for home with their ''weather report.''

Due to lack of fuel and replacement parts for their aircraft most of the Luftwaffe was grounded by the middle of April 1945. The Allied fighter units took advantage of this position and sent out many strafing missions to destroy aircraft and their airdromes as well. Though some of the airfields were deserted and the planes unfueled, most were still manned, and the flak batteries as active as ever. Such was the airdrome that Major Edward B. Giller and members of the 55th Group attacked on the afternoon of April 16.

''Since the number of targets in the area (Brunnthal airdrome) was not lucrative enough to engage the entire squadron, I released the flights to find their own targets,'' stated Giller. ''I broke my White Flight down into elements to cover this area. My wingman, Lieutenant Arnold, and I made our passes parallel with the autobahn, from south to north, clobbering the aircraft which were parked in the woods along either side of the road. My first attack was on a Heinkel He 111; I gave it a pretty good squirt and observed many strikes. It started to burn in a beautiful burst of flames.

"Parked just beyond the He-111 was an Me-109. I put the pipper on it, getting a good concentration of hits. Just as I pulled up, a steady stream of black smoke began to belch forth from it.

"I had seen two other aircraft parked in this same area on the east side of the road during this first pass, so I went in again, making the same pattern from south to north. The first aircraft turned out to be a Junkers 52 parked a little farther back from the road than my first two targets. I fired at it, pretty well covering the engines; it burst into flames. I had to make a third pass to position myself on the fourth target which I had observed. It was a Ju-88. I came in on the same pattern, and although I observed many strikes, it would not burn. As I pulled up from this last pass, a 20mm flak shell came in the left side of my canopy and

Late-war markings are shown to advantage on this D model of the 353rd. No invasion stripes and full nose coverage of the black and yellow checkerboard were typical by 1945.

Another ace's mount, "Old Crow" was the trademark of Major C. E. "Bud" Anderson of the 357th Group. Anderson's combat aircraft were all named for the popular scotch, from a P-51B to an F-105D. (Anderson)

exploded, wounding me in the left shoulder. I was dazed and bleeding rather badly, so I called my flight together and went home.''

Thousands of German aircraft were destroyed in a similar manner during the final days of the Third Reich. As Allied tanks and troops pulled up to a standstill, P-51s continued to range over Germany until the very end.

The last Mustang victories in the ETO were scored on May 8, 1945, by Lieutenants Lee Larson and George Schroeder when they performed the unusual feat of destroying two Focke-Wulf 190s without firing a shot. The 15th TRS pilots approached the planes with the intention of escorting them back to base. The 190s took hostile action and the two Mustangs reacted. Schroeder followed one which hit the deck at a suicide altitude, and followed it until it crashed into the trees.

Larson fastened himself to the tail of the other. The 190 dived to 500 feet, made a tight turn to the left, spun out and crashed into the ground. The only shots were those fired by the Germans in their first hostile action. They scored a single hit in Schroeder's left wing.

A new P-51C assigned to the 370th Group as a transition aircraft during change-over from P-38s to Mustangs. The Ninth Air Force group moved into Germany late in the war, retaining this plane as a "hack." The red spinner and rudder stripe signify the 485th Squadron. (Meryman)

From December 1943 until V-E Day on May 8, 1945, the Mustangs had taken the war to the depths of Germany. They had fought the best that the Luftwaffe could put into the skies and beaten it down to the ground. Not a square foot of the defeated Third Reich was safe from their guns and bombs. The high-pitched whine of the Merlins sang a song of victory as the silver Mustangs headed home from their last day of combat over Europe.

CHAPTER 5

THE EIGHTH AND NINTH VS. THE GERMAN JETS

The appearance of German jets in 1944 came as no great surprise to Allied Intelligence. Since 1943 it was known that the Luftwaffe possessed such craft and was striving to make them operational. The Messerschmitt 163 (actually a rocket-driven interceptor burning hydrogen-peroxide and water with hydrazine hydrate and methyl alcohol for a catalyst) and the Messerschmitt 262 had been in development for two years, and RAF photo-reconnaissance had been keeping tab on their bases for some time. The initial test of the Me-262 had been so successful that General Adolf Galland, Chief of Luftwaffe Fighter Forces, had requested that other fighter production be curtailed in order that more resources and attention could be devoted to the craft. Unfortunately for the Luftwaffe, and fortunately for the Allies, Hitler decreed that the Me-262 be developed as a bomber! This resulted in at least a four-month delay in making the aircraft tactically operational, much to the chagrin of the German fighter pilots.

Colonel Avelin P. Tacon, Jr. was leading his green-nosed 359th Group Mustangs in the vicinity of Merseburg, Germany, on the 28th of July when he encountered two Me-163s. One of his pilots called out two contrails heading for the bomber stream, so Tacon put his flight into a 180-degree turn to meet the interceptors head-on. Once the Mustangs were sighted, the Me-163s split up, one diving rapidly toward the ground and the other pulled up into the sun, his rocket engine blowing defiant smoke rings at the pursuing Americans.

The impact of this encounter is indicated by the following extract from a TWX sent out by Major General William Kepner, Commander of the VIII Fighter Command, the same day:

    . . . . IT IS BELIEVED THAT WE CAN EXPECT TO SEE MORE OF THESE AIRCRAFT IMMEDIATELY AND THAT WE CAN EXPECT ATTACKS ON BOMBERS FROM THE REAR IN FORMATIONS OF

The shape of things to come: Messerschmitt's revolutionary 262. Though at least 90 mph faster than the P-51D, the German jet was slow to accelerate and was vulnerable at low airspeeds. Mustangs claimed 118 Me-262s in aerial combat.

WAVES. TO BE ABLE TO COUNTER AND HAVE TIME TO TURN INTO THEM OUR UNITS ARE GOING TO HAVE TO BE IN POSITIONS RELATIVELY CLOSE TO THE BOMBERS TO BE BETWEEN THEM AND OUR HEAVIES. IT IS BELIEVED THESE TACTICS WILL KEEP THEM FROM MAKING EFFECTIVE, REPEAT EFFECTIVE, ATTACKS ON THE BOMBERS. ATTENTION IS CALLED TO THE FACT THAT PROBABLY THE FIRST THING SEEN WILL BE HEAVY, DENSE CONTRAILS HIGH AND PROBABLY 30,000 FEET AND ABOVE APPROACHING REAR OF THE BOMBERS. JET AIRCRAFT CAN ESPECIALLY BE EXPECTED IN LEIPZIG AND MUNICH AREA OR ANY PLACE EAST TO NINE DEGREE LINE.

General Kepner was not the only one excited about the event. The appearance of the jets brought VIII Bomber Command face to face with a new dilemma. Would the escorting Mustangs be able to cope with all-out attacks from the new aircraft, or would their speed present such a problem that bomber losses would again become prohibitive? This was the moot question of the day and the greatest test of combat which had ever confronted the indomitable Mustangs!

The problem was intensified with the first real success of the German jets on August 5, 1944. On missions flown that day, the VIII Bomber Command lost three aircraft to the new threat, and in an attempt to protect the bombers, three Mustangs fell victim to Me-163s. The rocket-fighters came down on them from above in trail and pressed their attacks to point-blank range, then zoomed into the sky above. The three P-51s of the 352nd Group caught fire and fell earthward.

On August 16 a Mustang registered its first kill over one of the new Luftwaffe aircraft. Lieutenant Colonel John B. Murphy of the 359th Fighter Group was flying escort in the Leipzig area when the bombers came under attack from Me-163s. One of the tiny craft cut his power and dived upon a straggling B-17 and Murphy pushed everything to the firewall to try to close the gap. Although he was indicating over 400 mph, the jet still had time to overshoot the bomber before the Mustang got his chance.

As the Me-163 flattened out of its dive, Murphy opened fire at 1000 feet and closed to point-blank range, getting strikes on the tail and left side of the fuselage before he overshot and had to pull off to the side. His wingman, Lieutenant Cyril Jones, closed in and took a shot from slightly beneath and the enemy fighter split-essed and headed down with Jones still getting strikes. However, he hit the wash from the rocket and blacked out, so they had to settle for a damaged claim on the enemy plane.

The initial victory was not long in coming, for when Lieutenant Colonel Murphy pulled out of his climbing turn, he sighted another Me-163 circling off to his left, 5000 feet below. Diving down, he came inside the circle of the jet and fired, closing rapidly. Hits on the left side of the fuselage caused a large explosion and the rear of the fuselage blew off. The Mustang had scored its first triumph over a jet!

Most jet contacts up until October 1944 had been with the rocket-powered Me-163. At the insistence of Reichsmarshal Hermann Goering and fighter commanders in the Luftwaffe, two Jager-Erprobungskommandos of Messerschmitt 262s were formed under the able leadership of Major Walter Nowotny, a 250-victory ace. A total of some 30 aircraft were assigned to the unit, based at Achmer and Hesepe near Osnabruck, Germany.

An ill omen for the Luftwaffe and sign of the tactics to come was demonstrated by a Mustang pilot, Lieutenant Urban L. Drew of the 361st Fighter Group on October 7. On this day he caught two Me-262s taking off from their base at Achmer, and using his advantage of speed and altitude, dove down on his prey to destroy both of them.

That same day, American fighter ace Colonel Hubert Zemke, who had immortalized himself flying P-47s as commander of the famed 56th Fighter Group, chalked up an Me-262 while flying a Mustang. Zemke, who had recently taken over the 479th Fighter Group of the Eighth Air Force, encountered an enemy aircraft while flying in spotty weather in the vicinity of Nordhausen. Zemke and his wingman, Lieutenant Norman Benolt, attacked what they thought was a Messerschmitt 109.

They obtained good strikes at long range and the left wing of the craft broke off in a dive at 520 mph at 10,000 feet. On their return to base they filed a claim for the destruction of an Me-109 shared. Evaluation of their film definitely identified the aircraft destroyed as an Me-262, and not a propeller-driven plane as originally believed. So, unknowingly, the two pilots had become early victors over the vaunted German jet.

The superior high-speed performance of even a lone Me-262 was demonstrated in a wild-and-wooly encounter on the afternoon of November 1. The B-17s of the Eighth Air Force had been on a mission to the synthetic oil refinery at Gelsenkirchen with little opposition, and were on their way home via Holland when they were intercepted by Oberfahnrich Banzhaff. Approaching at 38,000 feet, the Luftwaffe pilot nosed his plane into a dive toward the top cover section of Mustangs from the 20th Fighter Group. Down he came in a perfect dive and quickly he lined up the fourth P-51 in the formation and shot it down in flames.

Banzaff continued his dive over the Fortress formation with Mustangs in hot pursuit. Leveling out at 1000 feet, Banzhaff made a climbing 180-degree turn at full throttle, taking up a northerly heading toward the Zuyder Zee, just above a cloud layer. Had he ducked into the clouds he would have gotten off scot free, but he apparently decided that his superior speed was enough to see him through. This was a fatal mistake, for it gave an assortment of Mustangs and Thunderbolts from three different fighter groups a chance to cut him off.

Both types of aircraft opened fire on him, getting hits on the left side of the fuselage and the left wing. Lieutenant Dick Flowers of the 20th Group got strikes in his screaming Mustang, which was pulling 72 inches of mercury at 3000 rph, as did Lieutenant Gerbe of the 352nd Group. Once the jet had made the mistake of letting the Americans catch him, there was no hope to outmaneuver them. In desperation, Banzhaff made a climbing turn to the left and Lieutenant Groce, a 56th Group P-47 pilot, easily pulled his nose right through the jet in order to get enough deflection, firing all the time. The right engine burst into flames and the jet fell off into a spin. The pilot bailed out.

Six pilots had been involved in downing the 262, but it was subsequently awarded to Mustang pilot William Gerbe and Thunderbolt pilot, Walter Groce, on an equal basis.

In view of the superior speed of the Me-262, the Mustang pilots quickly realized they must develop new air-to-air tactics. Altitude and maneuverability were essential countermeasures. To engage the jet, the P-51 needed to initiate a diving attack to gain closure speed on the enemy aircraft. Only in this manner could the Mustang pilots get in striking range of the jets when they attacked the bombers. If attacked, the P-51 could easily maneuver inside the turning radius of the Me-262. This put the Mustang in a position to meet the jet head-on or to get in a shot if the enemy overran in his attack. The P-51 pilot was actually in a much better position to defend himself than he was to divert the swift attacks of the jets upon the bombers.

Kommando Nowotny saw its last action on the eighth of November when it lost four aircraft, including its leader. At least three of these fell to Mustangs, Lieutenant James W. Kenney of the 357th Fighter Group was escorting a fellow pilot who was experiencing engine trouble back to England when they met a formation of unescorted B-17s. Kenney decided that if his comrade's aircraft could make it, they would tag along with the bombers for a short time. During this period, Lieutenant Franz Schall in his Me-262 attacked the Fortresses and came back past the P-51s. Kenney turned to the attack and was able to get in a good burst from a 90-degree position as the jet came winging past. Strikes were registered all over the jet's left wing and engine.

At this time Schall reported to his ground controller that his throttles were jammed; apparently he didn't realize that his engine was smoking badly. Struggling to regain power, he glanced back to discover two Mustangs sitting on his tail. Fully realizing his hopeless plight, he chose to jettison the canopy and hit the silk.

Another Me-262 was shared by two Mustang pilots, Captain Ernest C. Fiebelkorn of the 20th Fighter Group and an unidentified flier, possibly from the 357th Group. Just as both pilots lined up for the kill, the jet spun in and exploded without either firing a shot.

Perhaps the most decisive Me-262 loss occurred when Major Nowotny went down in flames. It is known that he attacked a formation of bombers and that he in turn was intercepted by Mustangs. His last radio transmissions reported, ''Just made the third kill . . . Left jet has failed . . . been attacked again . . . been hit.'' Seconds later his Me-262 came screaming down and crashed in flames six kilometers north of Bramsche.

After this air battle, General Adolf Galland gave the order to dissolve the Kommando for reorganization. During the period of October 1 to November 8, 1944, the unit had been credited with the destruction of 22 Allied aircraft.

The remaining pilots of the unit were to form the nucleus of the first jet fighter wing, J.G. 7, which would be led by another high-scoring Luftwaffe ace, Major Theo Weissenberger. By late December it was in position as I/J.G. 7 at Brandenburg-Briest; II/J.G. 7 at Neumunster and III/J.G. 7 at Parchim.

Although few jets were encountered for the balance of 1944, fighter commanders were aware of the problems that these aircraft would present to the bomber formations good flying weather began to prevail. One such commander who was hard at work on a solution to the dilemma was Lieutenant Colonel William C. Clark, who had just taken over the 339th Fighter Group of the Eighth Air Force.

With the able assistance of some of his veteran pilots, Colonel Clark began researching all possible information relating to the Me-262. Where and how they were built, where they were based and how pilots were trained, where their fuel came from, etc.

Then the three known air bases of the jets were selected for special study. Photos of the fields provided valuable information concerning the general terrain and defenses, and best low-altitude approaches were determined. The general idea was to flush the 262s and shoot them down as they attempted to take off. If the jets refused to rise to the bait, then the air bases would be strafed and as many planes destroyed on the ground as possible. In addition, the bases would be shot up to such a degree as to render them unserviceable.

One squadron of Mustangs would be left high in the air as top cover for the strafers if any airborne Me-262s got away. Another flight of eight Mustangs would loiter in the area to get any escapees who tried to come home to roost.

In the spring of 1945 Colonel Clark was to put these tactics to use with great effect. To what extent is best described by Clark. ''Of the three air bases we picked, we were able to attack two. Of the first (just northwest of Berlin), we claimed and were awarded three destroyed and two damaged in the air. We found out later that we had chased six more north to the Baltic where they flamed out and were lost. We never got credit for these, of course. One more tried to land at the base after our last flight had left but flamed out off the end of the runway and crashed.

''The air base was so badly damaged that it never became operational again. I inspected it myself after the war and found that no repair work had been done after we left it. A Luftwaffe officer told me that we set their fuel supply on fire and they could get no more. Two Me-262s which survived the attacks were put in storage.

''We didn't lose a single airplane on this operation. I am more proud of this fact than anything else. On three planned missions (March 20, March 30 and April 3, 1945) we were credited with eight destroyed, one probable and five damaged in the air; 26 destroyed on the ground, and we probably caused the destruction of that many more without a loss of our own.''

The effectiveness of catching the Me-262s on takeoff is expressed in the combat-encounter report of Captain Donald M. Cummings of the 55th Fighter Group, who got two on February 25, 1945.

''I was leading Hellcat Yellow Flight on a fighter sweep at 10,000 feet in the vicinity of Giebelstadt airdrome when several Me-262s were called in at two o'clock, taking off from the field. Captain Penn, the squadron leader, ordered us to drop our tanks and engage. I peeled off from 10,000 feet, making a 180-degree turn to the left in a 70-degree dive after a jet which was then approaching the airdrome.

I commenced firing from 1000 yards in a steep diving pass, and after about three seconds observed many strikes. Since I was closing fast and approaching the airfield, which was beginning to throw up intense and accurate flak, I broke left and up, taking evasive action when about one-third of the way across the field. My wingman, who was behind me, saw the 262 touch ground, cartwheel and burn.''

The last claim against the erratic Me-163 was scored on March 15, 1945, in the Leipzig-Kassel area. Captain Ray S. Wetmore of the 359th Group was credited with a Komet when it attempted to intercept the bomber stream. It was Wetmore's 17th kill in Mustangs, raising his total to 21¼.

While the Me-163s gained much publicity, it is doubtful that they downed over a dozen Allied aircraft during the war. The extreme danger of operation of this rocket-powered plane and its very short endurance in the air handicapped the Me-163 etensively.

Mustangs continued to encounter and harass Me-262s as the war in Europe drew near an end. Major Edward B. Giller was among those who caught one of the jets trying to return to its home base. On the afternoon of April 9, 1945, Giller sighted a 262 at 24,000 feet in the Munich area. Two other Mustangs took off chasing him, and after about ten minutes Giller managed to cut him off after the other two gave up the chase. He stayed with the jet as he began to let down south of the city.

''I lost him again for a minute, then discovered him making for Munich/Riem airdrome,'' Giller recalled. ''I didn't know if he was going to land or try to drag me over some flak. Going 'balls out' I caught him at 50 feet just over the perimeter track. He was going west to east about 100 yards to the right of the runway. I fired several bursts and observed strikes on the leftwingroot and fuselage. I noticed his wheels were not down and his airspeed was about 200 mph. As my speed was about 450, I overshot rapidly and pulled up. When I looked back, I saw him crashland or belly in on the field 100 yards to the right of the runway in a large cloud of dust and flying pieces. He did not burn, which I believe was due to the fact that he was out of fuel. The aircraft was completely wrecked.''

Lieutenant Colonel Jack W. Hayes took the 357th Fighter Group's P-51s on an escort mission to Pirna on April 19, and returned to hide in the sun over Ruzyne airdrome at Prague, Czechoslovakia. After playing the cat-and-mouse game in the clouds for a few minutes, Me-262s were seen to begin taking off two by two. The bounce was made after 16 of the jets had become airborne. In the ensuing combat, four 262s were destroyed and three damaged.

Lieutenant Colonel Hayes got strikes on the 262 leader who turned left, hit the deck at full power and crossed the river at the southern outskirts of Prague. Here Hayes encountered intense and accurate flak from the ground. Still hanging on, the Mustang pilot lost the jet temporarily behind a tall building on the eastern shore of the river, and as he pulled up over the building, he saw the 262 hit the ground in a sharp turn to the right and slide into a building.

Perhaps one of the most frustrating combats by a Mustang pilot with one of the Me-262s was experienced by Lieutenant Theodore W. Sedvert of the Ninth Air Force's 354th Group. On March 2, 1945, Sedvert observed a 262 drop a bomb on Osthofen. Holding altitude advantage, he dove down to do away with the intruder. Good strikes were obtained in the tail and fuselage of the Messerschmitt. As it attempted to flee, it began to lose power and slow up. Sedvert pulled in, fired the rest of his ammunition and the jet still flew along. With no more rounds for his guns, the P-51 pilot pulled up alongside the 262 and peered across the way into the cockpit of his opponent. To add insult to injury the German pilot had the gall to thumb his nose at him.

Sedvert figured that was the limit to the whole thing. He pulled his .45-caliber pistol from its holster and blazed away. Still no visible effect! However, as he continued to fly along, the 262 began to smoke and he watched the pilot belly it in near Wiesthal.

Late in 1944 another German jet made its apperance. This was the Arado 234 twin-jet reconnaissance bomber. However, it tended to make only brief hit-and-run strikes and proved no match at all for the Mustangs which got it in its sights.

The first jet bomber in combat was Arado's 234, rated at 530 mph. It entered combat in July 1944 and could carry 4,000 pounds of bombs, but the type was deployed only in small numbers. At least a dozen fell to P-51s. (Wright Field)

Lieutenant Colonel John C. Meyer accounted for the first Ar-234 en route to his ranking as second highest-scoring Mustang ace. Meyer and George Preddy both flew blue-nosed P-51s of the 352nd Group. (USAF)

The first of this type to fall victim to a P-51 was shot down on December 31, 1944 by Lieutenant Colonel John C. Meyer of the 352nd Fighter Group.

Few piston-driven German fighters were to be seen in the skies by March and April of 1945. All priority had been given the Me-262 jets, and several new groups of these fighters had been formed. In January of 1945 the most elite unit the Luftwaffe had ever known was organized under the command of General Adolf Galland. Ten of the pilots in Jagdverband 44 were holders of the coveted Knights Cross, and most were high-scoring aces who had seen years of combat flying.

Even this did not deter the success of the American P-51s in racking up victories. On the tenth of April the American bombers were violently opposed over Germany

John Meyer's personal Mustang, "Petie 2nd," showing 18 of his final 24 aerial victories in WW II. Originally CO of the 487th Squadron, he eventually commanded the 352nd Group. (USAF)

by the jets, who took a toll of ten of the four-engined craft. However, they lost 20 of their own number, 18 falling to the guns of Mustangs. In one of the combats, a 262 made a rare head-on pass at the P-51 flown by Captain Gordon Compton of the 353rd Group. Compton gave him a short burst and the Me-262 burst into flames. The pilot bailed out and cleared the plane, but his parachute never opened.

The German jets and the Mustangs continued to mix it up until the very end of the war, but the Luftwaffe's new planes had come along in too little quantity and too late to inflict the damage that they were capable of doing. Formations of P-51s over the jet bases had made operations extremely hazardous for the German pilots, and even the presence of FW-190s as takeoff and landing cover was in vain.

The Mustangs from North American may have been outclassed in speed, but when it came to maneuverability and tactics, the steed came through with flying colors.

CHAPTER 6

RAF AND FRENCH MUSTANGS

Mustang Is and IAs continued in service with the RAF during 1944, but in decreasing numbers. Several of the squadrons converted to later models of Spitfires and Hurricanes, but six remaining units kept their Mustangs after D-day. Number 2 Squadron became the first unit in western Europe to receive the newer Mark IIs, which they took to France in July for operations with the Second Tactical Air Force.

In the course of operations with Army co-operation units, pilots flying the Mustang Marks I and IA claimed a total of 33 enemy aircraft destroyed. The most successful squadrons were No. 400 RCAF, with 11 victories and 414 RCAF, with 10 enemy aircraft credits.

Few early Mustangs saw service in the Mediterranean area, but during April 1943, 225 Squadron operating in Tunisia received four F-6B tactical-reconnaissance

An excellent view of the Mustang Mark IA. This cannon-armed model was used for ground support and interdiction. (RCAF)

A Mustang I, with dive brakes extended, prepares to nose over with a pair of 500-pound bombs.

This well-used Mark I belonged to Number 26 Squadron at Duxford, the "South African Squadron" which traced its origin in 1914 to the first aviation unit formed in that part of the Commonwealth. (RAF)

Mustangs from the USAAF, which it used in the final stages of the North African campaign.

The P-51B and C Mustangs equipped with the Packard-built Merlin V-1650 engine went into service with the RAF as Mustang Mark IIIs. A total of 274 P-51Bs and 636 P-51Cs were delivered to the RAF, with initial deliveries going to the squadrons of No. 122 Wing based at Gravesend. Numbers 19, 65 and 122 Squadrons received their aircraft during January and February 1944.

_ The British pilots were enthusiastic about the Mustang III, especially its range, but were very disappointed with the side-hinged, integral cockpit canopy. As quickly as possible this was replaced with a bulged clear blister, similar to that fitted on the Spitfire and known as the Malcolm hood after its designer. So successful was this modification that many examples of the hood were acquired by units of the USAAF in England, where they were at a premium with the pilots.

The new RAF Mustang Wing began operations late in February of 1944, escorting U.S. heavy bombers as well as U.S. and Royal Air Force medium bombers. Many fighter sweeps were carried out, and it was on such a mission that the wing's initial aerial combat took place. The three squadrons were flying the Strasbourg-Nancy area of France when 14 enemy fighters were encountered. Flight Sergeant Basilios Vassiliades of 19 Squadron latched onto an Me-109 and shot it down while the wing leader, G. R. A. McG. Johnston and Flying Officer Mutter of 65 Squadron each accounted for one. The wing lost one Mustang in the action. The next day four aircraft of 122 Squadron arrived over an airfield at Dole/Tavaux, near the

Close-up of the Malcolm Hood, fitted to many P-51B and C Mustangs. Its bulged contour actually allowed pilots to look aft, under their tailplanes.

Swiss border, and caught a formation of eight Heindel 111 bombers. Six of them
fell to the guns of the Mustangs, two by Flight Lieutenant L. A. P. Burra-Robinson.

During March and April of 1944, three more squadrons were equipped with
Mustang IIIs; Nos. 129, 306, and 315, the latter two being Polish units. These
squadrons formed 133 Wing at Coolham under the command of famed Polish
fighter ace, Wing Commander S. F. Skalski. Another Polish squadron, No. 316,
was also re-equipped and was based at Coltishall.

Both RAF Mustang wings were very active in June of 1944, giving fighter cover
to the Allied beachheads on Normandy, strafing and dive bombing enemy troops
and communications. Number 133 Wing was active on June 7 when No. 306
Squadron attacked 30 Me-109s near Beuzeville, shooting down five of them plus
three probables for the loss of three of their own. On a later sortie over Dreux,
more 109s were encountered, with 306 Squadron claiming six shot down and two
probables. Number 315 Squadron tapped four and Number 129 got one at the loss
of one. Squadron Leader E. Horbaczewski had led 315 Squadron on a successful
attack against German tanks in the region south of Cherbourg on June 22, when
the Mustang piloted by Warrant Officer T. Tamowiez was shot down by flak.
Horbaczewski saw the Mustang make a forced landing in a marsh and decided
to see if he could help out. The Polish ace noticed some Americans preparing an

The D-Day campaign placed a premium upon tactical airpower, and maintenance
crews worked tirelessly to keep enough aircraft operational. (RAF)

emergency landing site, and though it was far from ready and still quite short, he managed to set his aircraft down on it. Immediately he borrowed a jeep and headed for the marsh.

Horbaczewski had to wade through water up to his chest, but he finally managed to get to the crash, extricate the pilot and drag him back to the jeep. When they returned to the landing strip, Tamowiez was told to sit in the seat and his commander crawled in and sat in his lap. Then, despite the condition of the strip, the Polish pilot got airborne and headed back to England.

On the last day of June, Wing Commander Skalski led a formation of 20 Mustangs to bomb a target northeast of Paris. Just as they were diving to drop their bombs, some 60 Messerschmitt 109s and Focke-Wulfs arrived on the scene, hoping to hit the Poles as they pulled out of their dives. However, the Mustang pilots managed to get rid of their bombs and began to climb to meet the attack head-on. As they did, the German attack broke up and small dogfights took place all over the sky. Skalski pulled in behind two of the German aircraft and gave them a short burst. Instead of breaking in the same direction they broke into each other! There was a tremendous explosion and then a skyful of debris was all that marked the spot where the two had flown.

Early in July of 1944, 133 Wing and 316 Squadron were switched from an offensive to a defensive role. They were ''loaned'' back to Fighter Command to help defend England against the V-1 attacks which were being launched at the

An oil-streaked Mustang III of Number 309 (Polish) Squadron shares ramp space with a Ninth Air Force B-26. In all, 20 RAF squadrons flew Mustang Mark IIIs and IVs. (Havelaaf)

rate of over a hundred bombs a day. The wing took up station at the landing ground at Brenzett, about ten miles south of Ashford in Kent and two miles inland from the coast. Number 316 Squadron was assigned to Friston near Beachy Head.

Because of their longer range and great endurance, the Mustangs were used mainly on the French coast and flew two-hour patrols, while the Spitfires and Tempests flying inland, flew one-hour patrols. These Mustangs were equipped with the Rolls-Royce "66" engine which at 3000 rpm and 68 inches of mercury developed about 1650 horsepower. A special fuel (130 octane) was used along with internal engine adjustments to increase the intake manifold pressure from 66 to 81 inches of mercury. At full throttle the average Mustang so equipped could hold about 420 mph at 2000 feet. The average speed of the first hundred V-1s shot down by the wing was 370 mph. The Mustangs performed quite well for this duty, the only difficulty being caused by the experimental fuel they were using.

Number 133 Wing was credited with downing 190 V-1s during its defensive tour, but there were times when unusual problems were encountered. Such an event took place during the first "doodlebug" patrol of a young Canadian pilot named Fred Holmes. "There was a shortage of fighters that day, so single aircraft were placed on patrols, usually covered by pairs of aircraft," recalls Holmes. "The ceiling was low, with rain, and doodlebugs came over steadily all day. I found myself patrolling from Beachy Head to a point east of Hastings alone and was

This Mark IV was flown by Flight Lieutenant Joe Doley of 19 Squadron. One of the RAF's premier fighter units, Number 19 transitioned from Spitfires to Mustangs in 1944. (Doley)

given a V-1 to find at an altitude of 2000 feet, but this was 300 feet above the broken cloud base.

"I was lucky enouth to find myself just behind and below this bird over the sea, and between clouds for long enough fo fire and see strikes on it before it bobbed into the clouds again. I dropped below cloud and waited for it to come out, but noticed that I was then right over the sea-front promenade of the city of Hastings — and the V-1 came out of the clouds, too. It was losing height and flying under control but obviously damaged.

"A few seconds before, I had wanted nothing so much as to shoot it down, now I wanted it to stay up and fly on and I sat just below it, throttling back, trying to reduce speed and get behind it, but it was losing power and slowing down as much as I was. As It got lower it squeezed me between itself and the rooftops. When the ground dropped away as we crossed a slight ridge, I got out from under and the stupid thing crashed into a field and exploded a block beyond the last row of houses."

Week after dreary week, 133 Wing continued to fly patrol against the V-1s. The pilots tired of the monotony of these missions and begged to get back into action in France. In order to boost morale, the wing was allowed to permit each of the squadrons to fly tactical missions over France one day a week in support of the Allied ground troops.

It was on such a mission that 315 Squadron gained another great victory on the 18th of August, but lost its gallant leader. Squadron Leader Horbaczewski led his unit on an independent fighter sweep over France in the Seine district to see if he couldn't get the Luftwaffe to come up to do battle, and they obliged. The Mustangs made landfall at 9000 feet, flew on to Carmeilles and then to Romilly-sur-Seine where they were to go down and strafe airfields. Near Beauvais some 60 German fighters were sighted in the air and the Poles attacked immediately. In the ensuing melee the Mustangs shot 16 FW-190s from the skies and only took one loss, but what a loss it was — Horbaczewski didn't return from the mission. His wingman saw him blast two 190s from the air, but nobody saw the leader get hit or go down.

The Mustang units remaining on the Continent throughout the summer of 1944 gave excellent support to the ground forces in France. Of particular note was the work of the RCAF tactical-reconnaissance Mustangs. Flying at altitudes of 200 to 6000 feet, these pilots provided infantry and armored units with excellent vertical and oblique photographs of the terrain and enemy installations. This work was often accomplished in the face of heavy enemy opposition. On July 4, Flying Officers L. F. May and J. L. Roussell, with J. C. Younge flying top cover, were on a reconnaissance mission over Dreux, when they were bounced by 12 FW-190s and Me-109s. May and Roussell became involved in a wild dogfight and Younge dived down into the fray. Younge immediately lined up an FW-190 and blew it up. The enemy seemed to lose heart in the fight and broke off the engagement. The three Mustangs successfully completed their mission.

By the beginning of December 1944, sufficient new Mustangs were available to equip five more squadrons in England. From these was formed the bomber-escort force of RAF Bomber Command. Some of these units later received P-51Ds, or Mustang IVs, as they were known to the RAF.

An amusing incident of this transition period is told by Squadron Leader F. E. Dymond who was then a young officer just phasing onto Mustangs. ''One unusual feature of the Mustang came in ground handling. One had to push the stick fully forward to unlock the tail wheel before executing a sharp turn. This procedure was completely alien to the nature, especially for a Spitfire pilot, because such a movement coupled with a burst of throttle would have smartly had the tail up in the air and probably the machine on its nose! One often saw the 'new boy' struggling to swing his Mustang around in dispersal, one wheel locked, stick hard back and lots of throttle, doing his best to pull the tire off the tail wheel which stubbornly refused to caster.''

During this period of late 1944, the first French unit began its transition to Mustangs. In January of 1945, Tactical Reconnaissance Squadron 2/33 of the French Air Force took its F-6Cs and F-6Ds over Germany on photo-mapping missions. The French command wanted to do its own crossing of the Rhine River in its sector, and all reconnaissance of the area from Mayence to Switzerland was done by this unit, which was doubly equipped with the F-6s and Lockheed Lightnings. This squadron literally became the ''eyes'' of the French forces up until the end of the war.

Once the RAF Mustang escort force got into action in the spring of 1945, they, too, began to encounter the German jets on their missions. Flying Officer ''Slops'' Haslop, an Australian flying with 165 Squadron, was among the few to down a rocket-powered Me-163. This action is vividly described by Fred Holmes, who was in the air during this combat.

''We had half-a-dozen Me-163s hanging around above us over Leipzig on April 10, 1945, on a clear blue day when you could see the snowcapped Alps. One of these craft darted at the bombers, and finding itself being cut off by a section of four Mustangs, rolled over on its back and headed straight down, hoping its speed would take it out of danger. Flying Officer Haslop was in one of those four Mustangs, and he didn't take his eyes off that 163, not even for long enough to look at his airspeed indicator. It might have distracted him. He got the diamonds of his gyro gunsight onto the rocket plane and fired once. The 163 pulled up sharply and 'Slops' tried to follow it but blacked out completely and partially lost consciousness until the black turned to gray and he could see again.

A French F-6D over the Alps. The Free French Air Force used these recon Mustangs during 1945. (Cuny)

"He gulped like mad to ease the pressure pain building up in his ears and turned to his altimeter to figure whether the 8000 feet indicated was 8000 or 28,000 — the last figure being where he had started from. The machine felt odd and so did he, so he set course for base, flying no faster than was absolutely necessary.

"What we saw from above as Haslop went down was the 163 pulling out of its dive into about four loops and then spinning off the top of the next one and going down and down until it exploded on the ground. We lost sight of the Mustang and were quick to inquire back at base as to who had got the 163. Haslop was identified as the culprit, although he hadn't been seen since, and almost half an hour after we had landed and the sky was quiet, we heard another Mustang flying carefully home. It landed so quietly and gently that we could have bet that the pilot had a headache — and he had, for when Haslop got out of it and saw how much higher its wing tips were above the ground than those of its neighbors, he began to understand that exceeding the aircraft's maximum permitted speed could be dangerous."

The RAF Mustangs were in action in western Europe up to the very end. On April 16, 1945, Numbers 442 and 611 Squadrons clamed their first Mustang victories when they encountered a bevy of FW-190s while escorting 20 Lancaster bombers to Swinemunde, where they sank the German pocket-battleship *Lutzow*. Number 442 Squadron got the last RAF Mustang victories early in May when they destroyed two Ju-88s.

In March of 1944 the first Mustang IIIs arrived in Italy and were assigned to 260 Squadron. In the Mediterranean Theater the RAF Mustangs were almost exclusively relegated to ground strafing and dive-bombing missions, at which they excelled. A second RAF squadron and No. 3 RAAF Squadron were all operating Mustangs before the end of hostilities. In early 1945 these units got into action using 60-pound-rocket projectiles with which they raised all sorts of havoc with German transport and supplies.

At the end of the war in Europe, the RAF took delivery of 600 Mustang Mark IVs at Dum Dum Airport near Calcutta for use against the Japanese in Burma and beyond. However, these came too late. Some 300 Mustangs had been assembled when the surrender came to the Asiatic Theater. Most regrettably, all of these Mustangs were scrapped shortly after V-J Day.

The Mustang really sold itself to pilots of many nationalities as well as to the Americans. Perhaps one of the greatest tributes to the Mustang was given it by the men of the RAF who had come to love the Spitfire.

"No pilot was ever more loyal to his aircraft than the Spitfire pilot, and no one was surer that he flew the finest aircraft that had ever been built. If anyone was going to find fault with the Mustang, these men would. Apart from some short-lived consternation about a structural weakness revealed by dive-bombing operations a couple of months later, they found no fault. The only machine the Mustang could not outfight was the Spitfire, but it offered many advantages in speed, range, comfort, ground-handling characteristics and stability on instruments that the Spitfire pilot never knew. Rather to their surprise, they liked it.''

CHAPTER 7

MEDITERRANEAN MUSTANGS

In a sense, the Mustang had been introduced to the Mediterranean Theater of Operations in the spring of 1943 by the USAAF's 27th and 86th Fighter-Bomber Groups flying the A-36. However, when the new Fifteenth Air Force was activated as the strategic air arm in that theater, two veteran Spitfire units received their first P-51Bs and Cs. Both the 31st and the 52nd Fighter Groups were transferred to the Fifteenth

Early P-51Ds bear candy-stripe tail markings of the 31st Fighter Group in Italy. Originally flying Spitfires, the group received Mustangs in the spring of 1944. (USAF)

from the Twelfth Air Force and were equipped with Mustangs, in which they would gain their greatest fame on bomber escort missions.

The 31st was the first to see action when it took the bombers to Turnu-Severin, Rumania, on April 17, 1944. They returned an exuberant group of men, acclaiming the range and performance of their new craft. Only five days later they really won their Mustang spurs on an escort mission to the Ploesti-Bucharest area in Rumania. While part of the group engaged 30 enemy fighters heading for the bombers, the balance of the P-51s bounced another 30 Luftwaffe planes, getting a real surprise jump on them. In the ensuing air battle the 31st shot down 16 of the enemy, for a loss of four of their own. When the full total was added, another seven probables and ten damaged were added to the score.

In May of 1944 the 52nd Group got in action with the P-51 and on the 27th of that month, a third Mustang unit was added to the roster. The veteran 325th Fighter Group, which was already a charter member of the Fifteenth AF, traded in its P-47s and flew its first mission in the new plane.

To the 325th fell the honor of escorting the B-17s on the first shuttle mission to Russia which was designated "Operation Frantic Joe." A top-secret mission had been slated, and all of the pilots anxiously anticipated just what kind of show it would be.

"The morning of June 2, 1944," relates Colonel Chet Sluder, who led the Checkertails, "we got 64 P-51s off and met the bombers and escorted them until we were well into Russia. I had been unable to get any decent maps for the trip

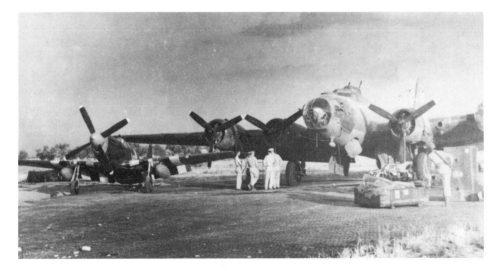

The P-51's exceptional range made it ideal for the long-distance shuttle missions to Russia. Here a visiting Mustang sits on a steel mat with a B-17 during a stopover in Italy. (USAF)

and was navigating off three sections, each of a different scale and color sceme. I was able to identify the Dneiper River, where I left the bombers and headed for Piryatin. The bombers went on to Poltava and Morgorod.

"The Ukraine was covered by a solid overcast at about 2000 feet, which made navigation a little more difficult, although the visibility was good below the clouds. This part of Russia is flat and featureless, so I had to fly strictly by compass. Piryatin was supposed to have a DF station to help us find the place, but I called several times and never heard a word from them. After holding my course for quite a time I realized that I had passed the field, so we did a 180-degree turn, thinking I would fly back to the Dneiper and follow it back into Kiev. In a few minutes I saw a 2½-ton American truck on the ground and a couple of Russian P-39s and forthwith landed at Piryatin!

"We were given a welcome by the American contingent and the Russians. In their debriefing hut, there was a complete selection of the latest air-navigation charts. It's too bad they hadn't been available in Italy."

The 325th flew one mission from Russia. On the morning of June 6, while Allied armies were hitting the beaches in France, their Mustangs escorted B-17s to the

Notables of the 325th Fighter Group meet Russian airmen during a shuttle mission. Group CO Chet Sluder shakes hands while aces C. J. Hoffman, Wayne Lowry, Bob Barkey and Roy Hogg look on. (Barkey)

airfield at Galatz in Rumania. Sixteen enemy aircraft were encountered and six of these were shot down, with the loss of two American fighter pilots.

After five uneventful days of no further operations, Lieutenant General Ira Eaker ordered the American planes back to Italy. The Checkertails mixed it up with a bevy on Me-109s on the way home and added three more victories to their banner.

The ex-Spitfire pilots of the 31st and 52nd groups were continuing to enjoy their successful transition. Captain Jim Brooks recalls some of the events and early combats during this period with the 31st Group.

"We checked ourselves out in the aircraft without any prior knowledge of its capabilities, other than what we could read from the tech orders. In other words, we combat tested the P-51 ourselves. Although the Eighth Air Force had been the recipient of these aircraft several months before we received ours, we still had no knowledge of just what the Mustang would do.

"One particular mission stands out in my mind, during the first few hours we had flown the P-51. I was leading an element to Munich, climbing at 25,000 feet when I spotted approximately ten fighter-type enemy aircraft off to my right and high. These aircraft were approaching us and I called to my flight leader to break right, which meant into the oncoming fighters, but he said later that he did not hear me. To make a long story short, I ended up all alone among these aircraft.

"It is also interesting to note that it seemed to be a mixed force; there were FW-190s, Me-109s, a Macchi 202. They had me hopelessly outnumbered. One FW-190 had his gear down, for what reason I don't know; however, he did make a head-on pass, firing as he came. He was of little concern to me at the time because the Macchi 202 had latched onto me and wouldn't turn loose. The radius of turn of the Macchi is better than the Mustang and we went around about three turns in a Lufbery circle. I knew that the fourth or fifth turn he would be able to pull his nose around and be in a position to fire, so I split-essed and fortunately he did not follow.

"Believe it or not, I climbed back up again and got back into the fight I had just left. However, I didn't stay around too long. At this time I figured that I had pretty well had it, so I headed for Switzerland hoping that if they did shoot me down I would be in Swiss territory and be interned. Fortunately, they soon gave up the chase and I returned to my base a very frightened, but a much wiser combat pilot. At this time I had only about ten missions."

Since being equipped with the Mustang, the 52nd Group had been getting appreciable scores on each mission enemy aircraft were encountered. On their mission to Munich on June 9, they found the bomber formations scattered and under heavy attack. Flying into the opposition, the yellow-tailed P-51s broke up the enemy concentrations and proceeded to blast 14 out of the air.

Second P-51 unit in the 15th Air Force was the 52nd Group, transitioning from Spit-fires in May 1944. This yellow-tailed, red-nosed Mustang flew with the 4th Fighter Squadron. (USAF via Simmons)

By June 23, the 52nd Group had set a Fifteenth AF record by downing 102 enemy aircraft in a period of 35 days. The 52nd's losses were under five per cent of the destruction inflicted on the enemy.

Late in June the all-Negro 332nd Fighter Group gave up is P-47s and converted to the Mustang. With their transition, the Fifteenth AF now possessed four P-51 groups which, in conjunction with the P-38 units, would escort the bombers until the end of the war.

One of the outstanding young pilots of the 52nd Group was Captain J. S. "Sully" Varnell. While escorting the heavies to Ploesti on July 9, Varnell and his top cover formation sighted some 50 Me-109s starting to dive on the bombers. "Sully" went down to the attack and shot down the tail-end Charlie of the 109 formation. Reefing around, he sighted another 109 and chased him right over the target area and flamed him in the midst of flak and falling bombs.

Varnell made a fast 180-degree turn to get out of the target area and sighted another 109. After his first pass, the German plane began to smoke and stream glycol, but it continued to fly. Varnell pulled around in a tight circle and came in again. A short burst right up the rear of the Messerschmitt and the German plane went down for good. "I'm getting 100 per cent on these claims," said Varnell in his debriefing. "I saw all three of them crash."

Another 52nd pilot who had a big day in July was Lieutenant Calvin D. Allen, Jr. who celebrated a real American-type Fourth. Leading an attack on a large formation of Me-109s that day, he tacked onto tail-end Charlie and got him with his first burst. Still in a dive, Allen slid behind victim number two, tapped him and then got a third before he had to pull out. As he zoomed up, the belly of a fourth Messerschmitt crossed his sights, so Allen raked him from stem to stern and down he went. Four on the Fourth is good in any pilot's book.

One malfunction that the Mustangs had been experiencing was rectified to the satisfaction of many pilots during July. There had been some trouble with cooling flap motors malfunctioning, which would permit the flaps to go to the full closed position. This caused overheating which brought on engine seizure. Some pilots had managed to literally "pump themselves home" by using the primer switch. One of the crew chiefs of the 325th Group came up with a spring-loaded tele- scoping rod. If the coolant temperature got too high, the pilot could pull the rod and force the flap open once more. This modification probably saved a number of pilots a long walk home or a stay in a German prison camp.

More confident than ever in the capability of their Mustangs, the pilots of the Fifteenth AF continued to demonstrate their prowess against the Luftwaffe. Three pilots of the 325th sent three Me-109s down over Vienna on the afternoon of July 17 without firing a shot. Lieutenants Stanley L. deGear, Horace H. Self, Jr. and Edwin R. Williams streaked down on a formation of three Me-109s who were approaching the bombers. "Each of us had a Jerry lined up in our sights," Williams said. "The Messerschmitt in the center spotted us coming in on his tail and in a sudden bit of evasive action, he flipped over and went straight down between the other two. His wing tips struck those planes and all three crashed together. The air was filled with a mass of motors, wings and tails."

On July 22, the 31st Fighter Group went to Russia as part of a task force composed of the P-51 unit and the 82nd Fighter Group in its P-38s. Over Rumania the Mustangs went down on the deck and strafed a number of enemy aircraft on the ground before proceeding to Piryatin.

On the morning of July 25, 39 P-51s took off from Piryatin to escort a P-38 strafing mission against Mielec Airdrome in Poland. The P-38s flew at 2000 to 3000 feet to the target while the Mustangs ranged some 5000 feet above them. The trip was uneventful and the Lightnings conducted a very successful strafing mission.

Once off the target, the P-51s left the P-38s to wind their way home alone. At 1345 hours, the 31st sighted a large formation of German planes cruising along, bomb-laden and headed for an attack on Russian ground forces. There were 36

Gathering of the Clan. The Checkertail Clan posed for this formation shot with a D model leading three Bs. Tail and wingtip markings are shown to advantage. (Checkertail Clan)

dive-bombers, four transports and one reconnaissance plane in the gaggle. The Germans never knew what hit them. The Mustangs dived down and tore the formation to pieces, then proceeded to pick off the singles. When the smoke had cleared 27 pyres were left burning to attest to the ferocity of the attack. The 31st winged its way home to Russia.

The following day, the 31st escorted the P-38s back to Italy and scored further aerial victories in the Bucharest area in the process. During the course of the Russian shuttle, 37 German planes fell before the guns of the 31st without the loss of a single Mustang.

The Fortresses and Liberators of the Fifteenth Air Force continued to take advantage of the summer skies to carry out their strategic bombing of Germany, central Europe and the Balkans. The P-51s escorting them turned in exceptional feats against Luftwaffe opposition.

The 325th Group was in position over the bombers which were attacking targets in southern Germany on August 3, when some 35 enemy fighters were sighted

This Mustang lost half its rudder but still managed to make it home to Lesina. (Wilson)

diving on another group of heavy bombers about 15 miles to the east. Captain Jack Bond immediately took his squadron to help them out. The Mustangs went into the enemy formation full bore and broke up the attack.

In making his pass on one of the fighters, Bond lost his canopy, which blew off and struck him on the head, momentarily stunning him. Shaking his head and wiping the blood from his face, Bond continued to bore in and shoot the German out of the sky.

August saw the bombing campaign against oil targets reach its climax. While covering the bombers in the Ploesti refinery complex, Lieutenant Robert Goebel of the 31st Group had a harrowing and unusual experience. During the mission of August 18, Goebel found himself alone on the deck some 50 miles southeast of the target. "Large columns of smoke marked the target area and I was going to take them on my right as I headed for home," Bob related. "I didn't particularly relish the idea of recrossing this area alone and on the deck. My engine was running rough and it looked as though the fuel was going to be close. While I didn't like the low speeds involved in a long climb, I figured I'd be better off at altitude than on the deck. I began my climb and at about 5000 feet made an S-turn to make sure I was clear behind and low. I had just rolled back out on course when I heard a bang and felt the aircraft shake.

"I bent it around as hard as I could and then took a look and, sure enough, there were two Me-109s. We went round two or three turns and just as I was closing the gap to where I could get a shot, they rolled out and hit the deck, flying line abreast about 500 yards apart. As I closed on the one on the left, they both started a turn to the left. I wasn't having any of that because it would have put me between them and given the other one a pretty good shot at me. When I rolled out, they regained their original positions. Now I bagan to wonder how I could break it off without attracting a following. I started to slide over behind the one on the left again, but this time the other turned too quickly and almost passed over me, going 90 degrees to my direction of flight. We were going at full throttle and I knew that by the time he could reverse his turn, he would be pretty far back. I pressed home my attack then.

"Only two guns were firing, which meant that I was just about out of ammo. We came to a slight rise in the ground and he must have looked back at me because he flew right into the ground. Luckily, I was firing at the time and the gun camera made a record of the whole thing.

"The rest of the flight was anti-climactic. I never saw the other 109 again. It was a funny thing, though. When I looked the aircraft over to see where I'd been hit, I could only find a very slight dent along the top of the cowl that didn't look at all like a bullet mark. I have often wondered if the engine detonated from being so hot, just at the right time to make me break."

By the end of August, the great Ploesti oil complex had fallen to the advancing Russians. P-51s of the Fifteenth Air Force now had a chance to assist the Russians by going after the Luftwaffe in their area. On the morning of August 31, 48 Mustangs of the 52nd Fighter Group took off from Madna en route to strafe Reghin landing ground in Rumania. Flight over the mountains to the Danube River was at 15,000 feet, after which, two of the squadrons let down gradually to the deck while the third squadron remained at 14,000 feet as high cover.

At 1005 hours the two squadrons of P-51s swept in over the airdrome. They caught the field by surprise and it was loaded with aircraft. Back and forth they screamed like a swarm of angry hornets, cutting a reaper's swath across the landing ground. Some of the pilots made as many as 12 individual passes before they broke off and headed for home. When the 52nd gathered its forces and set course for Italy, 60 Luftwaffe aircraft lay destroyed on the ground. Four Mustangs didn't get back to Madna.

One of the few enemy planes that could give the Mustang a real battle over Europe was the Italian Macchi 202. Although Italy had long since surrendered, there was a group of Italians who continued to fight on with the Luftwaffe nearly until the end of the war. It was one of the Macchi 202s that fell victim to the leading ace of the Fifteenth Air Force, Lieutenant John J. Voll, on September 23.

"On our way home," Voll reported, "I saw a Macchi 202 through a break in the clouds and went after him. Going in and out of the clouds, as we were, I was

The travel posters mentioned "sunny Italy" but winter brought freezing temperatures which failed to halt continuous maintenance. (Checkertail Clan)

Weather as advertised; clear skies still saw much maintenance performed outdoors in the Italian campaign.

chasing his vapor trails rather than actually seeing him all the time, and then when I finally got into position to fire, I glanced behind me and there was another Macchi on my tail.

"I started firing, and although I only used 20 rounds per gun on the Macchi in front of me, it seemed as though I'd used up a hundred before my shots blew the cockpit apart and the pilot bailed out. I started to attack the other plane, but by this time another had joined the fight, and since the Macchi can turn a shade sharper than a Mustang, they soon had boxed me in. I got into a cloud and headed for home."

Another pilot who was lucky to get home late in October was Captain Armour McDaniel of the 332nd Fighter Group. The unit was strafing oil barges in the vicinity of Odestal when the bullets from Lieutenant Robert Friend's P-51 ignited the oil on one of the barges and the Mustang pilot was forced to fly through the flames. Luckily he came out without damage.

It was then McDaniel's turn to go down and he hit another barge that set off a tremendous explosion. The force was so great that it ripped the guns out of his wings. Nursing the sturdy craft home from the target, he managed to keep it aloft until he reached Naples.

With the advent of fall, poor weather conditions not only held the bombers on the ground, but when they did fly a mission, the Luftwaffe was reluctant to combat both them and the massive cloud formations. However, the 31st Group got into a mass of German fighters while escorting the B-17s to Brux on October 16. Major George T. Buck was leading the squadron assigned to pick up the third group of B-17s. On arrival over Brux, there were no bombers to be found, so Buck swung his fighters in a 180-degree turn and proceeded to retrace the route. After only a few minutes flight, a swarm of Me-109s was sighted flying in the vapor trails of a group of Fortresses, closing for an attack.

"We got a good bounce on them, so we attacked," stated Buck. "The flight lasted about eight to ten minutes and the squadron accounted for ten to 12 kills and about a dozen damaged. I got three and on the last one I was in prop wash and was flipped on my back. When I righted the P-51, I lined up on another 109, pulled my trigger and got one pop from one gun. I thought I was out of ammo, but found later my guns had jammed. The final estimate, after viewing all the film, was that there were 112 Me-109s in the formation. They never caught the B-17s."

On the afternoon of December 22, Lieutenant Eugene P. McGlauflin and Flight Officer Roy L. Scales teamed up to destroy the first Me-262 credited to a Mediterranean unit. The pilots from the 31st Group were flying 15 miles northwest of Passau near the Austrian-German frontier when McGlauflin sighted the jet.

"I probably saw the jet before any of the others," Said McGlauflin. "All of a sudden, I looked up and almost right in front of me was this stranger. I called over the radio, 'George, is that you?' 'Hell, no,' was the answer and then someone squealed, 'It's a jet-propelled.'"

"I sent the rest of my flight with the reconnaissance plane we were escorting, and with my wingman, Scales, took on the jet job. Neither of us had any idea that we would shoot him down.

"Three times the German dived down and then pulled up in a wide sweeping turn to the left. I was very much surprised to find that my Mustang could gain a little in the dives. After the first time, I took a chance that he would pull left every time he climbed and sure enough he did.

"Every time he started to climb, I would cut inside of him and because my circle was smaller, I could climb with him, so I came quite close — within 800 yards — and each time he crossed my sights, I took a shot. I didn't see any hits, but then at that distance it's doubtful that I could see hits anyhow."

"I was shooting at him, too," commented Scales. "On his third climb he started a level turn at 28,000 feet and almost headed into me. I was only 250 or 300 yards away and shot at him with about 20-degree deflection. I saw what seemed to be red flashes coming off one nacelle and wing.

"He leveled off for a moment or two and then started a dive. At about 5000 feet, he leveled off again and smoke, quite a bit of brown smoke, started coming out. The pilot bailed out. We were diving right on his tail — I guess we hit 600 mph at times. When I landed, my crew chief remarked that the paint on my Mustang was wrinkled, which means that the wings had buckled a little. That dive knocked my oxygen system out, so if he had gone up again, I wouldn't have been able to follow.

"That certainly was a beautiful-looking plane. Silver and very streamlined, with yellow nose, nacelles and tail."

Regardless of the capability of the new jet, the Mustang plilots looked forward to further encounters with the Me-262. When spring of 1945 arrived they would get their wish.

However, bad weather and reduction of targets handicapped the pilots of the Fifteenth AF in early 1945. The onrushing advance of the Russians had taken out many of their former targets in the Balkans, and it became more and more difficult for the bombers to find strategic targets.

When pilots went to briefing on the morning of March 24, 1945, they were elated to learn that they were going to escort the bombers all the way to Berlin. The 1500-mile round trip was a long and tiring chore, but to fly to the capital of the Third Reich was a thrill that the pilots from Italy had never hoped to attain.

An armorer of the 322nd Fighter Group loads .50 caliber ammo in red-tailed Mustangs of the 15th Air Force. (Weatherill)

Though some of the units met with no enemy opposition, the 31st and the 332nd Groups tangled with some Me-262s. By utilizing the diving speed and maneuverability of the Mustang to best advantage, the P-51 pilots were able to emerge victorious. On the mission, five of the eight victories were credited to the 308th Squadron of the 31st Group. Captain William J. Dillard took off after a 262 in a long screaming dive that wound up on the deck. Strikes were scored on the left engine of the jet, which began to smoke and flame. The pilot flipped over and bailed out.

Colonel William A. Daniel fired a long-range burst that sent a jet into a snap roll then caused the plane to explode. Lieutenant William M. Wilder hit an Me-262 in one engine and it flamed, the pilot going over the side. Once the Mustangs could get in a good shot, the engines of these early jets were extremely vulnerable and inflammable.

The pilot of the fourth 308th victim went over the side while Captain Kenneth T. Smith was still firing, and Lieutenant Ray Leonard got the fifth by flaming both its engines.

Lieutenant Roscoe C. Brown of the 332nd Group peeled off to attack the jets and found one on his tail. Feinting first to one side and then breaking to the other,

Brown got the 262 to speed by him. The Mustang pilot then closed on the jet and flamed it. The pilot parachuted to safety.

Flight Officer Charles V. Brantley got the second 332nd victory when he followed a 262 into a dive. He registered hits all over the jet and had to pull out. The Messerschmitt continued to dive right on into the ground. The group's third victory was scored in a similar manner with Lieutenant Earl Lane pumping lead into the German jet until it went down trailing black smoke and flame.

As the war in Europe came to a close, enemy aircraft became more and more difficult to find. Lieutenant Norman Skogstad of the 31st Group managed to find a bevy of FW-190s over the Prostejov, Czechoslovakia airdrome on March 26th.

Sighting six 190s taxiing for takeoff, the P-51s circled at about 10,000 feet, preparing to hit the enemy planes when they were barely airborne. Catching his first victim while the FW's wheels were still coming up, Lieutenant Skogstad fired and destroyed him. He dumped two more in rapid succession as all three burst into flames and crashed. Sighting another Mustang with a 190 on its tail, Skogstad fired a wide-angle deflection shot, hit him and sent him crashing into the ground.

The guns of Fifteenth Air Force fighters were fired in anger for the last time on April 29, 1945. Mustangs of the 52nd Group dropped bombs on a highway and enemy convoy in northern Italy, while the P-51s of the Checkertail 325th strafed what targets they were able to find in the Udine area. Twenty P-51s escorted bombers of the 310th Bomb Group to drop leaflets on the third of May to close the books for the Mustangs in the Mediterranean.

In a little over a year since the first Mustang had been delivered to the 31st Fighter Group, P-51s of the Fifteenth Air Force had been credited with the destruction of over 1100 enemy aircraft in the air. The contrails of the escorting Mustangs of the Italian-based fighters had done much to emblazon the bridge of victory over the south of Europe and the Balkans.

The last moments of an Me-110 are captured on film as a Mustang closes in. (USAF)

CHAPTER 8

CHINA CHARGERS

The Mustang was introduced to Asia in the fall of 1943 with the arrival in India of the 311th Fighter Group under the command of Colonel Harry R. Melton, Jr. Its squadrons were equipped with A-36s and P-51As which were initially used for ground-support duties.

The first real test of the Allison-powered craft came in November of 1943 when the 530th Squadron was pulled down to Bengal to escort B-24s on a series of missions to Rangoon. For these missions the fighters staged out of Ramu, which was still 430 miles from the target. This was extreme range for the early-model Mustangs, even with drop tanks, which permitted them very little time over the target area.

The first of the missions was flown on November 25. Bad weather was encountered over the target and the problem was compounded by the appearance of Japanese Zeros which made determined attacks. The Mustangs managed to down one of them but lost two of their own.

Things were worse on the 27th when the P-51s flew the long route to escort bombers attacking the locomotive works at Insein. Resolute Zeros came up in droves to intercept and four Mustangs were lost, including the commander of the 311th, Colonel Melton. Four Zeros were claimed.

Two more missions were flown during these long-range operations, and the 530th found itself greatly depleted with a total of eight aircraft missing, due either to enemy action or lack of fuel. It had been a most disheartening initiation for the Mustang pilots, but the P-51As just didn't have the range or performance and the pilots had run up against some of the best Japanese pilots in all of Asia. However, things would get better. Of nine victories credited to the 530th Squadron in the November combats, two each went to Lieutenants J. J. England and R. F. Mulhollen. Both were future Mustang aces.

Other Mustangs began to arrive in the theater during this period. The veteran 23rd Fighter Group in China received its first P-51s in November and the 1st Air

Two P-51s of the First Air Commando Group above the rugged Burma mountains. (USAF)

Commando Group arrived in India equipped with P-51As. Both units put their Mustangs into action at once, with primary emphasis on bombing and strafing missions.

The Air Commandos' first big assignment came when General Wingate carried out his air invasion of Burma in early March of 1944. One of the more outstanding missions during that time was a strafing attack on the Japanese airfields at Anisakan, Burma, on the eighth of the month. Lieutenant Colonel Grant Mahoney, a veteran of early fighting in the Philippines and Java, led a 21-plane fighter sweep against the target.

Each of the Mustangs carried a large drop tank and a 500-pound bomb. On arrival in the area, Mahoney sent the eight P-51s, which would act as top cover, in first to bomb and strafe the antiaircraft positions. When they had made their runs, he set up his bombing-and-strafing pattern. Screaming down to the attack, the Americans placed their bombs on the Japanese revetments and fuel dumps. Then Mahoney climbed up and directed the strafing runs. Back and forth like bees after honey, they buzzed until all 35 enemy planes on the field had been destroyed.

The XX tail code identifies this P-51A as part of the 529th Fighter-Bomber Squadron. The photo was taken over Assam in March 1944.

The top cover Mustangs were kept busy, too. After dropping their bombs and climbing to altitude, Lieutenant Colonel Robert T. Smith sighted 14 Japanese fighters heading in to attack the strafers. Immediately he led his flight to intercept and even though his guns jammed he continued to turn into the fighters until the attack was broken up.

Captain Erle Schneider was even more determined. Closing on one of the Japanese fighters, he hit the gun tit until the plane burst into flames. However, in his concentration, Schneider had run in too close. Violently he pulled up, but his wing chopped the tail off the Japanese plane and the P-51 went spinning through the air out of control. This tragic act of the American pilot so demoralized the Japanese that they broke off the combat and scattered.

As time passed and P-51Bs and Ds arrived in the theater, the Mustang pilots began to give the Japanese a drubbing, no matter what type of fighter they encountered. One flight of six Mustangs of the 23rd Fighter Group encountered over 10 Oscars while pulling out of their 350 mph dives on a bombing mission near Tungting Lake on June 18, 1944. By staying close together during the first enemy pass, they were able to protect each other and get far enough away from the Japanese to turn and come back into the fight in a more advantageous position.

Captain Lester Murray, an element leader, pulled up from his bombing run and saw a green Oscar coming down on his flight leader. He had a 90-degree deflection shot as the enemy dove but got in an accurate short burst and saw strikes on the engine. The Japenese flipped off to the left and down as the Mustang continued to climb. Captain Murray and his wingman circled wide and climbed into the sun.

Flying at 10,000 feet, Murray sighted eight Oscars in a loose formation some 4000 feet below, circling over the other P-51s and Japanese planes that were locked in combat. Diving on a black Oscar, Murray closed to 1000 yards behind, pulled out and lined up slightly below the bandit. The Japanese apparently never saw the Mustang as it pulled in to 500 yards before opening fire. Flames had begun to stream back from the Oscar's engine as Murray ducked beneath it and the rest of the formation. Murray and his wingman kept going on their course for home.

Lieutenant Lloyd Mace was also leading an element when the P-51s were attacked from above. Mace tagged onto an Oscar when they came down and followed him down in his dive. Bucking and buffeting, Mace held his fire until the Oscar began a sharp turn to the left, but saw Mace's tracers and began a turn to the right. Just as he was about to pass over the Oscar, Mace pulled his Mustang's nose over sharply and sprayed the Japanese fighter, which burst into flames.

A second flight of four Mustangs went in to begin a dive-bombing run when they were attacked from above by six Oscars. When the Oscar pilots found they couldn't close on the Mustangs during their dive, the Japanese chandelled up and circled until the P-51s started to climb. Then the Japanese dove again, but the Americans split-essed and hurtled downward, leaving the Oscars behind.

Lieutenant Jack Green had dived three times to lose the Japanese. This time he circled wide and began climbing, but before he could get more than 1500 feet, he sighted another P-51 half a mile to his left with an Oscar on his tail. Lieutenant Green closed to 300 yards and fired at about 10-degrees deflection as the Oscar went into a shallow turn. The only strike noted was a tracer lodged in the wing, but apparently the pilot had been hit, for the fighter chandelled up, then dropped off and fell into a gradual curve into the ground. The P-51s departed without loss to themselves, claiming three kills and a probable.

Even the superior maneuverability and diving speed of the Mustang was not infallible. Some of the Japanese pilots were veterans of years of combat and masters at air fighting. One of the more memorable encounters on record of P-51 pilots in China was a fight between four Mustangs and a lone Oscar pilot who was respectfully dubbed "The Coach." This Japanese pilot showed all the ability and character of a storybook flier, engaging four of our best pilots using the best tactics. The fight was finally broken off after five minutes when the Japanese pilot apparently got tired and went home. This was one Japanese pilot even the Mustangs couldn't defeat.

The main baiting tactic the Japanese used against the Mustangs was dropping a decoy several thousand feet below a flight to make himself obvious and look like a juicy target. Attackers would be hit by the remainder of the flight above.

it was found, however, that with the superior speed of the P-51 at least one pass could be made at the sitting duck with practical impunity. In some cases, even the speedy Tojo fighter was fooled into allowing more than one pass on this decoy. After one such successful attack on a decoy, the engaging pilots went on record with the following evaluation: "It is perfectly safe to attack a decoy in this fashion, especially if you have two to three thousand feet of available diving space below because the P-51 can accelerate and dive away sufficiently fast to get away from the top cover if given a short lead."

Maneuvering at high speed was also an occasional cause of regret for Japanese pilots. P-51s were able to coax the enemy fighters into a high-speed dogfight and keep up with nearly all maneuvers. However, it was found that to allow the speed of the Mustang to fall below 350 mph put the American pilot at a decided disadvantage.

There was one incident of an American pilot who found himself at a very poor advantage, to say the least, yet he downed his unwary opponent. This Mustang pilot escorted B-25 bombers to the target where he mixed it up in a dogfight and got hit in the aft end of the fuselage. As the coolant temperature began to climb and vapors filled the cockpit, the pilot headed low over the hills for home. The engine began losing power so the pilot jettisoned the canopy and unfastened his safety belt. Suddenly the engine stopped completely. The American had one foot on the wing and was ready to push off when he saw a Tojo fighter headed directly at him. The pilot squeezed the trigger for one quick burst. With this, the aircraft stalled out, throwing the Mustang pilot against the wing, but somehow he managed to pull his rip cord and drift earthward. Amazed, he saw the Tojo hit the ground and explode during his descent. The American was picked up by Chinese and returned to his base.

The Japanese began a great offensive in China in the summer of 1944 and the Fourteenth Air Force was extremely hard pressed to fly its many ground-support missions. Day after day the fighters and bombers of General Chennault's command ventured out to bomb and strafe the onrushing Japanese ground forces. Enemy fighters attempted to take advantage of the situation by attacking the Mustangs while they made low-level bombing-and-strafing runs.

The P-51s of the 23rd Fighter Group had been bombing and shooting up enemy barges in the Hengyang area on June 29, 1944 when they spotted a four-plane flight of Oscars, two silver and two green, at about 10,000 feet, flying good formation. One of the green Oscars immediately began dropping down as a decoy while the others covered him. Lieutenant Putnam dove on the decoy, making a head-on pass but getting no hits. One of the top cover Oscars dropped on Lieutenant Putnam's tail and Lieutenant Stanley Trecartin dropped on this craft and scared

A black-tailed P-51B of the 23rd Fighter Group taxies in after a mission. (Weatherill)

him off. Another Oscar came down on Trecartin but fired from out of range, and the Mustang, in a 20-degree dive, pulled away with ease.

By the time the Mustangs had pulled up to about 7000 feet the Oscars were back in their original formation, three above and one below at the same level as the Americans. Lieutenant Putnam proceeded to make a head-on pass on the Oscar decoy. Trecartin stayed out to the left about a half mile at the same altitude and watched. Putnam and the Oscar passed in their attacks and began 180-degree turns in opposite directions. This brought the Oscar into Lieutenant Trecartin's vicinity. Apparently the Japanese pilot didn't see Trecartin, for he cocked up in a vertical bank and must have blacked out for a moment.

Trecartin drove up behind him to 100 yards. The Oscar pilot then had a chance to see the P-51 when he skidded, appearing to clear his tail, but either did not see the Mustang or took it to be friendly. Just then the P-51 began to fire at the Oscar, which started to turn and was caught by a burst in the cockpit. The Oscar flamed immediately.

The three Oscars above either never saw the fight or chose to ignore it. They made no move to intervene and the P-51s left the area unscathed.

The Japanese continued to advance against an exhausted Chinese Army throughout the summer. The number of ground-support missions flown by the Fourteenth Air Force increased steadily, and at long last the cry for reinforcements began to be heard and new aircraft and pilots were rushed into the theater from the United States.

One of the new leaders who came to China was a 34-year-old veteran pilot who was destined to become the top fighter ace of the CBI. His name was Major John C. "Pappy" Herbst and he demonstrated to the younger pilots just how it should be done.

Herbst scored two of his early victories on September 3, 1944, when he went to the Tsienshan area to skip-bomb the railway bridge. Shortly after the bombs exploded, Herbst sighted two silver Val dive-bombers come out of the clouds. Apparently they were curious as to the rising column of smoke in the target area.

The major maneuvered behing the two Vals as they came down to 2000 feet, and exploded one on his first pass. The second one flicked down, and it was a chase as the maneuverable little dive bomber tried to make the P-51 spin in. Herbst went to work on him right away, shooting off part of the rudder and chewing up the aft fuselage despite the efforts of the rear-gunner. The Val attempted to land in a rice paddy, but nosed over on its back.

Two days later, Herbst got into his fiercest fight while on a routine cross-country to Kweilin to take his P-51C back for modification on the link ejection chute. A build-up of clouds and thundershowers was encountered on the mountaintops west of Kanchow, so he skirted around them to the north to come back south in the Saing River valley.

Just after passing Chaling, Herbst spotted two eight-plane flights of Oscars at 10,000 feet. They were apparently flying cover for an unknown number below, for he got a glimpse of some of them. Immediately, the California ace pushed his throttle to the firewall and gained some altitude in order to sneak in on the last element of the eight-plane flight furthermost to the east. Sunlight reflecting off the silver Mustang undoubtedly alerted the Oscars, for they turned into him level.

Herbst flew a head-on pass on the leader of the Japanese formation and saw him start to smoke as he blazed past. However, the Mustang took hits, which shattered the windshield and gave Herbst a faceful of glass. At this time, the westernmost flight of Oscars was coming in head-on!

Major Herbst concentrated on the leader once more and scored repeated hits before he had to break away. Blinded by blood and with only one gun firing. Herbst was fighting for his life. It now seemed that he was meeting attacks continuously. After one pass the P-51 pilot saw a parachute going down before him, so he knew he was giving a good account of himself. Finally, the single gun jammed. It was now or never, for the Oscars were queuing above him like a bunch of vultures ready for the kill. Slamming the stick forward, he dived downward. Steadily the needle moved forward on his airspeed indicator as he hurtled earthward. Pulling back at the last possible moment, he broke up and away, hurtling over the landscape. He had lost them in the dive. "Pappy" Herbst headed for home.

The Chinese Army had received reinforcements in the fall of 1944 and the tide of battle began to change. However, this meant no let-up in operations for the China Mustangs. They continued to harass the enemy in every way possible. On the morning of December 23, 1944, 16 P-51s of the 118th Tactical Reconnaissance Squadron under the command of Lieutenant Colonel Edward O. McComas were airborne from their base at Suichwan, China. The mission was to skip-bomb the Wuchang-Hankow ferry terminal. On arrival at the target two flights broke off to bomb and strafe the piers and tracks leading down to them. Both attacks were quite successful and the pier on the Hankow side of the river was left wrecked and burning.

McComas stayed above to lead the flight covering the fighter-bombers, and when their chore was completed, he took his Mustangs down to the deck to do a bit of strafing. A number of aircraft were sighted on the ground at Wuchang airdrome and in the course of several passes, McComas managed to shoot up a Lily and an Oscar.

As he pulled up from the field he sighted six Oscars above him. One of the enemy tailed him and managed to put some hits into his wing, but McComas dove away and lost him. Climbing to 7000 feet, he sighted another Oscar which he

Distinctive red and black markings identify these B models as belonging to the 118th Reconnaissance Squadron, based in China during 1944-45. (Lubner)

attacked from astern, getting good hits at the wing root. The Japanese pilot jettisoned his canopy and bailed out.

Two more Oscars jumped McComas so he headed southeast toward Kiukiang and managed to get away from them. As he passed over Ehur Tao Kow airfield he saw nine Oscars preparing to take off. He circled the field and made a west-to-east pass on two of the planes just as they cleared the runway. He fired into the closest Oscar and it flipped over and crashed into the other and both plowed into the ground just east of the field.

McComas then pulled up behind two other Oscars just after they took off abreast. Closing to within fifty feet of them, he fired a long burst into each. Both were seen to crash east of the airfield.

Four days later "Pappy" Herbst got his 13th and 14th victories while leading the first fighter sweep over Canton. South of Canton, Herbst engaged three Oscars which were diving toward some American fighters strafing below. Coming out of the sun and slightly beneath, he closed to within 50 yards of an Oscar which did not burn but rolled over and crashed into the Canton River.

One of the top-scoring P-51 pilots against the Japanese was Lt. Col. Edwin O. McComas, CO of the 118th Tactical Recon Squadron. Attached to the 23rd FG in China, McComas claimed 14 victories including five on 23 December 1944. (Rust)

Firing at the other two, which split in different directions, Herbst observed hits and closed on the aircraft which broke to the right. Another burst flamed the Oscar on the wing and around the fuselage. In the meantime, the other Oscar slipped in on Herbst's tail and chased him. Going "balls out," the Mustang managed to get enough distance between him and the enemy to permit a 180-degree reversal. The Oscar didn't go along with the head-on pass and broke, in an attempt to flee, permitting Herbst to get behind him. The P-51 closed the gap and Herbst managed to put some slugs into the Oscar before it got away to the west.

Enemy fighter opposition over China almost disappeared after January 1945. A few combats during the middle of the month brought eight victories, including Pappy Herbst's last three. But the 23rd Fighter Group claimed only two more shootdowns by war's end. The Mustangs continued to escort the bombers and shoot up the enemy on the ground, but dogfights with Oscars and Tojos belonged to the past. From defeat and disappointment in the early Mustang of 1943, the fighter pilots of the CBI had gone on to triumph with the later models of their China charger.

CHAPTER 9

PACIFIC PONIES

It was late 1944 before Mustangs made their appearance in the Southwest Pacific. First to arrive were the fighter squadrons of the 3rd Air Commando Group. These units were manned primarily by veterans of the air battle in Europe, and perhaps no more experienced fighter organization was ever committed to combat.

Had the Japanese still been giving the Americans a fight for the skies to any extent, they would have met some of the AAF's best fliers, but such was not the case. When the 3rd Air Commandos arrived in the Southwest Pacific, the action had passed far to the north, and not until they were finally moved up to the island of Leyte in the Philippines did they see any action. Even then, enemy aircraft were few and far between. The pilots were forced to concentrate on ground-support

F-6Ds of the 71st Tac Recon Group over the Philippines, 1945. (Krane)

strikes, and later they took to the air to bomb and strafe what limited opposition still existed on the island of Formosa.

Another unit that added some Mustangs to its force late in 1944 and early 1945 was the 82nd Tac Recon Squadron of the 71st Recon Group. At the time, the unit was based on Mindoro in the Philippine Islands. Most of its work had been photo missions, and to get any aircraft fully fitted for fighting was something new.

On the morning of January 11, 1945 two pilots of the 82nd Tactical Reconnaissance Squadron went out to their Mustangs to prepare for what seemed a routine mission. The leader of the two, a slender young captain named William A. Shomo, was dropped off at his aircraft to begin a mission that would bring him undying fame.

The two Mustangs taxied out briskly and took to the skies, climbing on a northerly course that would take them to that portion of the island of Luzon which was still occupied by the Japanese. There, they were to photograph airdromes to ascertain whether the enemy was still utilizing them.

Lieutenant Paul Lipscomb was tucked in nicely on Shomo's wing as they sped over the countryside at only 200 feet. Just south of Baguio they sighted a twin-engined Japanese bomber with an escort of 12 Tonys some 2000 feet above them. With an escort like that, there just had to be a VIP aboard.

Up Shomo climbed to the attack, with Lipscomb right on his wing. None of the Tonys broke or maneuvered to intercept during the first pass, so either they

Cowlings pulled for maintenance, inspection panels open and armament bays ready. The 71st TRG takes a stand-down to keep its Mustangs in good shape. (Krane)

"The Flying Undertaker" flown by Major W. A. Shomo became the best-known Mustang in the Pacific after its pilot downed seven Japanese planes in one mission. (Winkle via Hill)

didn't see the Mustangs coming, or they mistook them for friendlies. Whatever the reason, the two Americans didn't miss. The bomber and one of the fighters fell on the first pass.

With this, the Tonys broke, but seemed confused and befuddled as to what to do. The Mustangs whipped in and out among them, knocking them from the sky, one by one. Nine of the Japanese fighters went crashing to earth before the remaining duo managed to break away and streak for home at full throttle. Shomo had not only done away with the bomber, but had six fighters fall to his fifties! Lipscomb had a real masterpiece to report also. Three Tonys downed in the brief scrap.

For this record feat, Shomo became the second Mustang pilot of World War II awarded the Medal of Honor. He had scored one victory the day before, to bring his total victories to eight.

The veteran pilots of the 3rd Air Commando had little chance to score in the air, but they did a fine job of ground support during the Philippine campaign. As the fighting in Luzon came to a close, their Mustangs began to fly missions against Japanese bases on Formosa. It was on one of these missions that Captain Louis E. Curdes had the most unusual experience of his World War II career.

Curdes was no stranger to combat. He had flown P-38s with the 82nd Fighter Group in North Africa and Italy, and had chalked up eight victories in the Mediterranean Theater.

On the morning of February 10, 1945 he and his flight of three were briefed to depart their base at Mangaldan on Luzon and make a reconnaissance sweep to the island of Formosa. From there they would proceed down to the Batan Islands and check out a small dirt strip on one of the islands which the Japanese reportedly were using to shuttle bombing missions against the Manila area.

The flight to Formosa proved uneventful, and after an hour of checking enemy activity and weather conditions, the four P-51s turned southeast. En route to the Batan Islands, two Japanese Dinah reconnaissance planes were sighted. Swiftly, the Mustangs sped to the attack and Curdes couldn't help but grin when the eager young pilots of his flight sent both of them splashing into the sea in less time than it takes to tell about it.

On arrival over the Batan Islands, Curdes dispatched two of his flight to search the southern half of the islands while he and his wingman took the northern section. Back and forth they flew fruitlessly, when his radio crackled.

"Red Three to Red Leader. We've found an airstrip down here and we're ripping it up. We've flamed three of their planes on the ground, but there are two left."

New P-51Ds of the 348th Group on the rugged island of Ie Shima stand by to use the coral runways. Originally the first P-47 unit in the Pacific, the 348th transitioned to Mustangs in early 1945. (Krane)

Quickly Curdes and his wingman banked hard to the south and throttled forward to join in the fun. About that time a call of distress came from one of the strafing pilots. He had taken a slug in the leg and his plane was badly hit. He would have to bail out. Curdes arrrived on the scene just in time to see a parachute settling into the shallow bay off the island.

He sent Red Four scurring for home to get air-sea rescue out, and dispatched his wingman up to altitude to send a distress call.

Curdes went down over the treetops and gave the ground installations a good working over with his guns until all was quiet, and then pulled up to survey the situation. From the north a twin-engined aircraft appeared. Apparently it was a C-47, but Curdes couldn't imagine what an American transport would be doing in his area.

Cautiously, he closed on the plane, and there, just as big as could be, was the white star on the blue background. Pulling in formation with the C-47, Curdes attempted to raise the crew on the radio but could get no reply. Lower and lower the plane descended, undoubtedly intending to land on the Japanese-held strip. In desperation he fired a burst across its nose, but oblivious even to this warning, the transport continued its descent.

Working around to the tail of the C-47, Curdes lowered his flaps and lined up on the port engine. Abruptly he pressed the gun button and watched with satisfaction as his slugs tore into the nacelle. He was rewarded with a stream of smoke form the riddled engine.

As quickly as possible, he slid in behind the starboard engine and repeated his performance. Now the C-47 lost altitude rapidly and the pilot lined up to ditch the aircraft. The plane hit the water, threw geysers into the air and reared to an abrupt stop. Dinghies were inflated, and as Curdes circled, he counted 12 Americans scamper out and splash into the rafts.

Curdes and his wingman continued to circle the dinghies until a relief flight of Mustangs arrived on the scene. They protected the floating survivors until nightfall. It was too late for the PBY flying boat to make the rescue.

The following morning the PBY picked up the crew of the C-47 plus the medical team, which included two nurses it had been transporting. Also rescued was the downed fighter pilot from Curdes' flight. The pilot of the C-47 had become lost, and little did he know how close he had come to delivering himself, his crew and the medical team to the Japanese.

For this action, Captain Louis Curdes was awarded the Distinguished Flying Cross; undoubtedly the only pilot to receive such an award for shooting down an American aircraft.

In the Southwest Pacific area, American Marines and Army infantrymen had been island hopping. Throughout the summer of 1944, island after island had been

Captain Louis E. Curdes of the 3rd Air Commando Group really got around the war. He shot down seven German, one Italian and one Japanese aircraft — and an American C-47! Actually, he was rewarded with a decoration for the latter, as he saved the crew from capture.

invaded and wrestled from the hands of the Japanese. The fall of Saipan and Tinian in the Marianas Islands to U. S. Marines set the stage for air bases to be built that would handle the massive four-engined B-29 bombers. The first Superfortresses began to arrive in October 1944 and the first preliminary missions against the Japanese bastion of Truk were flown on the twenty-sixth of the month.

On the morning of November 24, 1944 the first very long range mission set out for Tokyo. As expected, large formations of enemy fighters were encountered and they extracted their toll of the heavy bombers. They continued to go on subsequent missions over Japan, but there could be no turning back in the bombing campaign.

It was essential that the B-29s get long-range escort, but it was an impossible 1500 miles from the Marianas to Japan. Not until an island base closer to the Japanese mainland had been taken could fighter escort be provided.

On February 19, 1945 U. S. Marines landed on the island of Iwo Jima. In a tremendous and bloody battle the Marines initially secured enough of the area for a landing strip to be built. On March 6 the first Mustangs of the 15th Fighter Group landed on the island. Although Iwo Jima was not classified as secure, the pilots of the 15th came in to begin their operations from the South Field strip.

Safe bomber. The copilot's view from a B-29 as Mustangs ride in close on the way to Japan. (USAF)

Combat air patrols were started at once. These proved to be uneventful, but the weather was a constant problem during that time. On March 11, the group began flying neutralization missions against the islands of Chichi Jima and Haha Jima. Strikes were flown against the airfield, aircraft and shipping in the area. As a rule, few ships or aircraft were caught in the area, but the bombing and strafing of the airfield went on regardless.

The 15th was joined on the island by the 21st Fighter Group on March 23. These two units of VII Fighter Command teamed up to fly missions in the area which would prove such valuable training for the very long range (VLR) missions that began in early April.

The night of March 27 proved to be a grim and gory experience for the officers and men of the VII Fighter Command. In the early hours before dawn, bivouac areas awoke to small-arms fire and insane screams. The Japanese had stealthfully made their way past the Marine perimeter and broken into the camp area. They seemed to be everywhere, firing into tents, slashing them with samurai swords while laughing, screaming and shouting.

Confusion reigned. Men tumbled from their cots, scrambled for weapons and fired at point-blank range. Many had no weapons and fled for anything resembling shelter. One pilot managed to wrestle a saber away from a Japanese and choked him to death with his bare hands.

With the sounds of gunfire, the Marines rushed into the area with rifles and automatic weapons. Swiftly and efficiently, skirmish lines were formed and a combination of Marines and armed AAF personnel proceeded to clean out the pockets of the enemy. When it was all over, 333 Japanese bodies lay sprawled over the northwest corner of the island. Forty-four officers and men of the VII Fighter Command had lost their lives and 88 were wounded.

The big day for the Mustangs arrived on April 7 when they flew their first Very Long Range (VLR) mission. One hundred and eight P-51s took off from their bases on Iwo Jima and escorted the B-29s of XXI Bomber Command on an attack against the Nakajima Aircraft Engine Factory at Tokyo. Seventeen of the fighters had to abort on the long 660-mile trek to the Japanese capital, but the balance made rendezvous with the bombers at Kozu.

The Superfortresses flew in neat group formations of staggered vees as they headed in for the target. The P-51 units broke out of their loose squadron formations into flights of four and hastened to get above and to the flanks of their assigned bomber units. These were readily identified by the big, bold and black markings on the tails of the B-29s. Once dispersed, the flights of four began to weave, first one element in front and then the other. This enabled them to not only keep close watch on the bombers, but to protect each other's tail in case enemy fighters dived from above.

Ten minutes after rendezvous the Mustangs made landfall at altitudes of 17,800 to 20,000 feet, with the bombers at 15,000 feet. The first enemy fighters were encountered over Sagami Bay between Atami and Hiratsuka. Japanese fighters of all types flew to the attack; Nicks, Tonys, Tojos, Irvings and Zekes arrived in profusion. Most of them attempted to dive on the bomber stream from the front quarter and that's when the P-51s proceeded to go to town.

Major Gilmer Snipes was leading a strike of 20 Mustangs from the 45th Squadron, 15th Fighter Group, when the first bogies were encountered. He dropped his wing tanks and suddenly his engine quit for a full two minutes. He lost several thousand feet before he was able to get it started and fly back to the bombers.

An attempted pass on a Tony was unsuccessful, but then Snipes and his wingman sighted two Tojos flying line abreast. As they closed in on the tails of the Tojos and opened fire, Snipes got hits and saw his target begin to smoke. However, as the Mustang overran, the Tojo broke downward and was not seen again. Then another target came into the major's sights and he gave it a burst. One gear came

Zebra-stripe tails identify these Mustangs as 458th Squadron aircraft seen from the gunner's blister of a B-29. (USAF)

down on the Tojo, and then it began to come apart. The pilot was seen to bail out some two to three thousand feet below.

In the Tokyo area a twin-engined plane was seen to make a two o'clock run on the B-29s and drop a phosphorous bomb. Lieutenant W. E. Brown dove down to make a head-on pass and set the plane on fire. It was last seen spiraling downward.

Lieutenant Charles Heil became a one-man task force that day. Heil missed the three navigational B-29s flying with the Mustangs for the mission and joined three others headed for Nagoya — although this was unknown to him when he attacked on. At the rendezvous he sighted B-29s all over the sky, but no P-51s. Heil continued to fly with the bombers, thinking they were headed for Tokyo.

His engine began to act up as the bombers were turning on the bomb run. He contacted one of the B-29s and informed him that he could not continue with them. One B-29 dropped its bomb load, turning back with him. Three hours after landing at Iwo, Heil discovered that he had been to Nagoya instead of Tokyo.

The Mustangs shot 21 enemy aircraft from the sky that day and lost but one of their own, which exploded over the target area. On return to base, one pilot who was low on fuel bailed out over a rescue destroyer 200 miles north of Iwo and was immediately picked up.

High scorer for the day was Major James B. Tapp, who would later become the first ace of the VII Fighter Command Mustangs. He was credited with the destruction of four enemy fighters. He damaged a Nick on his first pass and then caught a Tony in a high-speed climbing turn. As he closed in and fired, hits were registered and the plane caught fire. Then it exploded with one wing ripping away and fluttering down like a falling leaf.

Tapp then observed a B-29 in trouble heading for the coast. An Oscar attempted to get to the cripple, but Tapp cut him off and shot him to pieces in a head-on pass. Tapp and his wingman then pulled in to give the Superfort close protection. This was disputed by four Zekes and two Tojos. The two P-51s barreled in, broke up the attack and Tapp blew the wing off one of the Tojos. The B-29 flew on unmolested.

There was much jubilation among the B-29 crewmen upon their return. Not only had their desire for revenge against the Japanese fighters been consummated, but they had witnessed the great difference that an escort of Mustangs could make.

The P-51s escorted the bombers again on April 12 and destroyed a further 15 enemy aircraft. Then on the 16th they flew the first of their fighter strikes, which would become more the rule rather than the exception for the balance of their VLR missions. The Mustangs had no trouble getting the B-29s to the targets, but the bombers just weren't getting the desired results from high altitude. General Curtis LeMay decreed that the majority of B-29 missions would take place at night

Ready to touch down on Iwo Jima after the long haul to Japan is a Mustang of the 45th Squadron, 15th Fighter Group. (USAF)

and that they would primarily drop their fire bombs on the Japanese targets from altitudes of from 9000 to 12,000 feet. These missions were so successful that daylight escort missions for the Mustangs were cut drastically. The P-51s were given the task of going after the Japanese airdromes.

The Mustangs fought the Japanese in the air and then shot up planes and installations on the ground. Great use was made of the five-inch rockets which were carried on twin zero-length launching stubs under each wing. These proved to be highly effective against aircraft and other inflammable targets.

Distance and weather plagued the Mustangs throughout these long-range operations. Jackknifed into the cramped cockpits, the P-51 pilots flew for eight or nine hours over 1300 to 1600 miles to spend a few minutes over the target. "It wasn't so bad after the first hour because your legs got numb," said one pilot. "But when you got home, you didn't feel much like sitting. You were raw."

On each mission, weather reconnaissance B-29s were sent ahead of the Mustangs to clear them to the targets. However, the weather on the mission of June 1 brought about the greatest tragedy to a P-51 mission which occurred during World War II.

That day 148 Mustangs of the 506th, 21st and 15th Fighter Groups were air-borne to escort the XXI Bomber Command on a maximum effort against Osaka. When the fighters reached a point approximately two hours from Iwo Jima, they entered a frontal area extending from the surface to 23,000 feet. Zero visibility, intense turbulence, heavy rain and snow scattered the P-51s so badly that it was impossible to maintain contact. Twenty-seven of the fighters broke out of the front and continued over the target, and 94 Mustangs returned to base. Twenty-four P-51s never returned from the mission.

In the "whiteout" conditions, undoubtedly there were collisions in addition to some of the planes becoming lost and flying until they ran out of fuel. Two pilots bailed out and were picked up by air-sea rescue vessels. Regardless, it was a sad and dejected group of fighter pilots who returned to Iwo Jima that day.

Air-sea rescue did a tremendous job assisting the Mustang pilots on the VLR missions. Navigational B-29s, Navy destroyers and submarines worked in con-junction along the mission route to pick up any fighter pilots who had to bail out or ditch along the way.

A fighter pilot who would attest to the virtue of ASR quite emphatically was Lieutenant Frank L. Ayres of the 15th Fighter Group. During the April 7 mis-sion, Frank bailed out 200 miles north of Iwo Jima after nursing his damaged fighter 500 miles away from Japan. He was rescued by a destroyer.

On June 23, over Japan, Lieutenant Ayres was a flight leader of the high cover for the fighter strikes on Shimodate airfield. He knocked down one Jap aircraft which he saw burn and crash, and followed a second fighter down to 6000 feet where he lost it in the clouds. His own plane was damaged in an ensuing fight with a Japanese plane which came out of a haze from above and riddled his engine.

Heading away from the target, his plane crippled and his radio out, Ayres picked up a reference point and steered for the area where he knew a lifeguard submarine was stationed. There he bailed out upwind of the sub, rolling the plane over and encountering no trouble getting clear. Remembering the difficulties of his first dip in the sea, he unfastened his chute straps before he hit the water. He landed about 100 yards in front of the submarine and didn't even have time to inflate his life raft before they tossed him a ring buoy and pulled him alongside.

Air-sea rescue services grew steadily during the course of the VLR missions. Before the end of the war as many as 14 submarines, 21 Navy patrol aircraft, nine navigational-and-rescue B-29s and five surface vessels would be spotted along the course of the bombers and fighters on a VLR mission. This service was a great morale booster for the Mustang pilots and certainly inspired them to greater tenacity in their air battles over Japan.

Dogged resistance to the P-51s by the Japanese fighters continued in the Tokyo area. As a result, VLR fighter strikes were increased in an attempt to break the back of this force. The mission of June 23 met with fierce and intense opposition which is best related by the official mission report of the 47th Squadron, 15th Fighter Group, which caught the brunt of the interception.

"Arrived at DP (Departure Point) at 1300 hours and turned to left toward Primary Target which was covered with clouds at 6000 feet. After four minutes on this course the squadron was tapped by seven Franks which made moderately aggressive passes. Lieutenant Colonel Thomas shot one down as did Flight Officer Jones. After receiving call from 78th Squadron that they were off target, the 47th Squadron went southeast toward Dasumigaura and were tapped by 17 Franks who came in for aggressive passes with altitude advantage. They made overhead, head-on and high side passes and attacked so suddenly that our pilots had no time to use mutual support and had all they could do to avoid their passes. Lieutenant Ayres and Lieutenant Burnett shot down two Franks and Lieutenant Scamara, Lieutenant Elliott and Lieutenant Baccus damaged four.

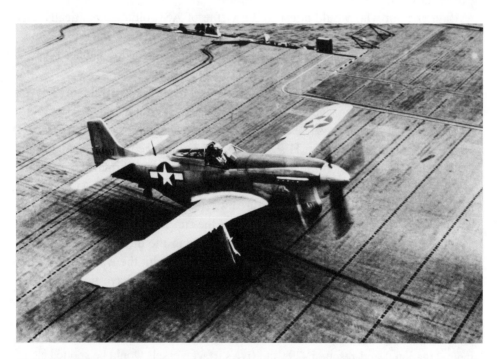

P-51D modified with a tailhook revs up aboard USS *Shangri-La* during carrier trials in 1944. The nautical Mustang would have been called the Sea Horse, but its use was not required. (USN)

"Our flights were pretty well disrupted in the dogfight that lasted about ten minutes. Lieutenant Worton attacked an Oscar from above and saw it hit the ground. Six Georges got on the tail of Lieutenant Scamara and Lieutenant Scanlan. Lieutenant Scamara shot down two and damaged two. Three Hamps attacked Lieutenant Oliver and Lieutenant Burnett, who then attempted to chase them, but they split-essed. Three Jacks were encountered by Lieutenant Worton and Captain Martin but they were unable to get any hits.

"A string of Jacks attacked Lieutenant Elliott and he dove to the deck pulling away from them. Lieutenant Elliott estimated that there were twenty-five planes in the string. Lieutenant Scamara and Lieutenant Scanlan were attacked by six Zekes from six o'clock above. Lieutenant Scamara managed to shoot down one Zeke and saw two Zekes on Lieutenant Scanlan's tail scoring hits. Lieutenant Scanlan's ammunition blew up and smoke started coming from his plane. Lieutenant Scamara attempted to help him but was not in position and at the same time was tapped again. Lieutenant Scanlan pulled away from the Zeros and bailed out. Lieutenant Scamara saw his chute open at about 6000 feet SE of Chosi Point over Cheba Peninsula.

"Lieutenant Christian was shot up by a Frank and Lieutenant Baccus led him toward rally point. He bailed out five miles N of the sub and Lieutenant Baccus got Maple Flight to orbit him in the water. He was later picked up by the sub."

The Japanese had proved they weren't out of fighters and experienced pilots, but the Mustangs had shown they could take on anything they had to offer and still outperform and extract a telling toll of them.

Two unusual strikes, one in the air and one on the ground, were flown by two Mustang pilots of the 531st Fighter Squadron on July 9, 1945. Captain Mathews, who was carrying a load of five-inch rockets under his wings, was faced by a head-on attack from four Tonys. He fired two rockets at them and missed. He then pulled up into the clouds and came back. He attacked one of the Tonys from the rear with his rockets. One of them hit the tail and went on past the plane, exploding in front of the Tony. The enemy craft was last seen spinning down into the undercast.

The ground attack was unusual in that the P-51 pilot, Lieutenant Thompson, attacked Itami Airfield alone. He had become separated from his wingman in an aerial scrap. Three passes were made. On the first he strafed a George fighter, and on his second pass he flew down to blow another George to pieces with rockets. Two more Georges were destroyed on the third pass by the Mustang pilot, who then set course for the rally point.

The VLR missions proceeded to take their toll of Japanese aircraft, and by late July the ratio of aircraft destroyed on the ground began to exceed those destroyed in the air. Although B-29s dropped the atomic bombs on August 6 and August

The Royal Australian Air Force acquired Mustangs late in the war. This P-51K flew with Number 84 Squadron, RAAF in 1945. (Pattison)

9, the Mustangs still went back to Japan on the tenth. On this, the final P-51 mission, escort was provided for the B-29s over Tokyo by the 15th and 506th Fighter Groups. Interception was made but six of the enemy were shot down by the pilots of the VII Fighter Command.

On September 2, 1945, Japan surrendered. World War II came to an end. The men of the Mustangs had proven that they could carry the war to the enemy in the Pacific as well as they had done in Europe. Once more they had been victorious over weather, distance, flak and fighters.

CHAPTER 10

POST WAR

The success of the P-51Bs and Ds brought many laurels to the North American stables, but there was no letup in development of further models of the Mustang during the war years. The lighter and speedier P-51H took its first flight on February 3, 1945 and showed signs of greatness. Although the new Mustang was some 700 pounds lighter than the P-51D, it had been strengthened structurally and it incorporated a new fuel system which lengthened the range appreciably. It was fitted with the Packerd-built V-1650-9 engine, which utilized the revolutionary Simmons automatic boost control for constant manifold-pressure maintenance and was equipped for water injection. With the use of the water-injection system it was possible to overboost the engine to develop a minimum of 2000 horsepower for a brief emergency period.

Although several thousand of the aircraft were ordered, multiple cancellations came with peace. Only 550 P-51Hs were built and none of them saw combat. The majority of these fine lightweight Mustangs did service with fighter groups in the United States and Alaska until they were replaced by jet aircraft.

Most fighter units overseas settled into the doldrums of occupation duty, and there was little excitement other than aircraft malfunctions. Such was an experience of Captain Wendell Hook, who flew the A-36 on many dive-bombing missions in the Mediterranean. Hook was operating from Johnson Air Base near Tokyo, flying the P-51K which differed only from the "D" model in that it was manufactured in Dallas and utilized the Aeroproducts propeller instead of the Hamilton Standard.

Hook was to lead a flight of Mustangs back to his home base at Itazuke when he experienced a propeller malfunction immediately after the wheels left the runway. "The prop went into full high pitch as it tried to feather itself," said Hook. "Of course it couldn't quite do that because of the stops. My wingman went zooming right by me. I had never had a power loss on takeoff, but there was the tachometer dropping rapidly and dragging the manifold pressure down with it.

The XP-82 Twin Mustang, a Packard-powered aircraft formed by two P-51s joined by a center wing section. (USAF)

"But the big V-12 never missed a beat with this terrible abuse (1200 rpm and 35 inches of mercury). I had maybe 50 to 100 feet of altitude, two 75-gallon external tanks nearly full, full internal tanks, guns but no ammo, minimum airspeed. I started a left turn, salvoed the tanks, called the tower for emergency landing, all in less time than it takes to tell.

"As I made the last turn onto a very short final, I could count every pebble in the dry rocky stream bed just off the runway. I nearly waited too long to put the wheels down, but I didn't really care how I landed just so I could walk away. Later it dawned on me that the hydraulic pump was running at half speed or less like everything else. The green light for the gear came only a split second before the wheels touched the runway!''

Although the fervent pitch of war had gone from flying, there were still emergencies such as these for the fighter pilots, and the faithful Mustang with its magnificent Merlin continued to bring them home.

Another latecomer in the Mustang line that would see considerable occupation duty was the P-82 or "Double-bird," as it came to be known to the pilots. In late 1943 design engineers realized that the extreme range of the Boeing B-29 would extensively tax the capability of the escorting fighter pilots who would cover the long-range missions with them. North American engineers went to work to come up with an aircraft that would not only have long-range capability but also would carry a second pilot who could share the flying duties.

The design basically incorporated two P-51H fuselages joined by a constant-chord wing between the two. A rectangular tailplane was used to join the empennage sections, and standard port and starboard wing sections were utilized as the outer wings. The pilot was housed in the port-fuselage cockpit and the copilot in the starboard. This unorthodox craft was powered by two V-1650-23/25 Merlin engines with counter-rotating propellers, and each main gear leg was attached to the front spar under the outboard side of each fuselage with wheel retraction coming inward under the fuselage and wing. Six .50 caliber machine guns housed in the center wing section constituted the P-82's primary armament.

Work on the XP-82 began in January 1944, and the first of two prototypes took to the air on April 15, 1945, by which time 500 production P-82Bs had been ordered. The end of the war on September 2, 1945, brought about the initial cancellation of 480 of these aircraft.

During 1946 the tenth and eleventh P-82Bs were fitted with large radar nacelles mounted under the center section of the wing and became night-fighter test aircraft. Procurement for that year was stepped up for the P-82s and some 250 were built; 100 as long-range escorts and 150 as night fighters to replace the outgoing P-61s. All of these planes were powered with the Allison V-1710-143/145 engines, and all night-fighter versions had modified the starboard cockpit for the use of a radar-intercept observer rather than a copilot.

One of the first fighter units assigned to the Strategic Air Command was the 27th Fighter Escort Wing which flew the F-82E. (In June 1948, all fighter planes in the U. S. Air Force were officially redesignated with the "F" for fighter prefix rather than the former "P" for pursuit prefix. Thus the P-82 became the F-82 and the P-51 became the F-51.) This unit made many long-range flights in the late 1940s, the most memorable being an over-water celestial navigation operation. Forty-four of the Twin Mustangs made a round-robin flight from Kearney AFB, Nebraska, to MacDill AFB, Florida, then on to Puerto Rico, Panama, Jamaica, Fort Worth, Texas, and back to Kearney. The longest hop was the 1600-mile jump between Jamaica and Fort Worth, with 1350 miles over water. For the conventional fighter planes of the day, this was quite a feat.

One of the squadrons flying F-82Es on night-fighter duty was the 449th, based at Adak in the Aleutian Islands. If ever a climate could bring out the worst in

F-82Es of the 27th Fighter Escort Wing, assigned to SAC, made the record-setting Caribbean round-robin flight. (Gers)

an airplane, it was there. However, for the most part the F-82s performed their job well. There were a few hairy moments, experienced when the only instrument inverter, which furnished electrical power for the flight instruments, went out. The aircraft, when first received, had all electrical instruments, and when the inverter failed, the pilot had to come in by the seat of his pants. A second inverter later look care of this problem.

At the end of the war many Mustangs were declared surplus and sold on the civilian market. These planes were modified in every manner imaginable and all sorts of record feats were sought in them, but the main event that caught the public's eye during the early postwar years was the performance of the Mustang in the revival of the famed Bendix Trophy Race. These California to Cleveland dashes were the highlight of distance racing in the 1930s, and the entry of World War II fighters into the field in 1946 was a natural.

As the starting date of August 30 approached, the veteran pilots worked feverishly to get the fighters ready for the flight. P-38 Lightnings dominated the entry list, with ten of the twin-boomed contestants. Other slated starters were two Bell P-63 Kingcobras, one Goodyear FG-1 Corsair, one Douglas A-26 and four P-51s. Highlighting the Mustang entries was a shiny brand-new craft which famed aviatrix Jackie Cochran had just received from the factory, and two Mustangs selected from a mass purchase by veteran stunt and movie pilot, Paul Mantz.

A primary consideration of all pilots in the race was fuel load for the distance, at an airspeed which would enable them to win. Permission had been granted to jettison drop tanks, but it had to be done over open country where no damage could be incurred. All of the flyers had been warned that any violation of this ruling would cost them their license. This stiff penalty cost several pilots considerable time in the Bendix Trophy races.

One of the first to experience drop-tank trouble was Jackie Cochran. When she attempted to jettison her oversize tanks, the front ends dropped and the rear held. This caused the nose of the tanks to drop down and kick the rear ends up into the trailing edges of the wings. Considerable damage was done before she finally got rid of them. Regardless of her difficulties, she was still able to blaze into Cleveland in 4 hours and 52 minutes, taking second place in the Bendix Race, 10 minutes behind Paul Mantz.

Mantz's blood-red Mustang, "Blaze of Noon," was the class of the field. Paul amazed the aviation world by removing the wing tanks from his airplane, sealing the wings up and filling them completely with fuel. This "wet wing" configuration, sans drop tanks, enabled him to cross the finish line in 4 hours, 42 minutes and 14 seconds, for top honors and the $10,000 prize money.

Actually all was not that simple for Mantz. When he raised his landing gear after takeoff, the sequence valve malfunctioned and the wheels folded up outside

Burce Gimbel flew this P-51B, owned by Jackie Cochran, in the 1947 Bendix Race. Gimbel finished fourth as Mustangs swept the first six places. (Reinert)

the wheel-well covers. Through some wild maneuvering he was finally able to get the gear down, and on second try the retraction was properly accomplished.

As soon as victory had been achieved, Mantz went to work on his Mustang to ready it for the 1947 competition. Once more the entire entry roster was filled with World War II aircraft and a challenge was hurled at Mantz by oilman Glen McCarthy's P-38 entry, "The Flying Shamrock." Vast sums of money were poured into the twin-engined fighter, to be piloted by ex-AAF captain Jack Ruble. The press gave considerable publicity to the personal bet between Mantz and McCarthy as to who would be triumphant in the race to Cleveland.

However, on the day of the race, "Dame Fortune" refused to shine on the P-38. Ruble experienced trouble from the beginning. He lost one of his drop tanks shortly after takeoff and was forced completely out of competition when one of his turbosuperchargers blew up over Arizona.

The real race developed between Mantz and another Mustang; "Magic Town" flown by Joe De Bona. Both pilots were airborne without mishap and poured on the coal in the race of their lives. Mantz thundered out of the west and set his Mustang down in the record time of 4 hours, 26 minutes and 57.4 seconds.

Mantz settled down to await the arrival of De Bona. His wait was short, and an excited roar came from the crowd as the Mustang streaked across the finish line. Now it was all up to the timers. When the result was handed down, De Bona clocked in at 4 hours, 28 minutes, 15 seconds. He had lost by only 77.6 seconds. For Mantz, it was another brilliant victory. For De Bona, a heartbreaking loss with only 1948 to look forward to. For the Mustang, it was another superb accomplishment; the speedy little fighter took all the first six places.

Paul Mantz repeated his win for the third time in 1948. For Joe De Bona, it was another excruciating loss for he had the race won up until the final few minutes. With the airfield in sight, his engine quit. He had figured his fuel too closely. In utter frustration he set the Mustang down in a cornfield only twenty miles from victory.

After three record-breaking wins, Paul Mantz chose not to enter the Bendix Race in 1949, but did enter two of his Mustangs which were flown by Harman "Fish" Salmon and Stan Reaver. However, this time Joe De Bona was not to be denied. Streaking cross country at high altitude, he crossed the finish line in only 4 hours, 16 minutes, 17.5 seconds for an average of 470 miles per hour. Stan Reaver took second place and Salmon third. It was another clean sweep for the Mustangs.

Accomplishment for the Mustang just seemed to keep growing during the five years after the war. Perhaps its zenith for these years was its Bendix Trophy triumphs, but many other records were being set by pilots in civilian status. One of the foremost was a speed record set by Jackie Cochran on December 12, 1947.

The famous red Mustang which Paul Mantz flew to victory in the 1946 and 1947 Bendix Races, averaging 435 and 460 mph, respectively. (Reinert)

Flying over a three-kilometer course, she clocked 412.002 miles per hour, a record which still stands for women in propeller-driven aircraft.

After less than five years of peace, world events took a sudden turn that thrust the United States into another conflict. It was time for the little record-breaking steed to step out of the winners' circle and its laudatory garlands and get back into warpaint.

CHAPTER 11

KOREA

In the wee hours of predawn on June 25, 1950, the North Korean Army launched an offensive into the Republic of South Korea. Sporadic incidents had occurred on the border at the 38th Parallel for some months, and initially there was doubt as to whether this was another hit-and-run raid or full-scale war. As the morning progressed and intelligence reports began to come in at the capital of Seoul, it was clear that this was no border clash. The North Korean Army was across the parallel and advancing all across the northern border.

U. S. Air Force units in Japan were alerted immediately and in view of the impending hostile environment, it was decided that all American nationals would be evacuated from the Seoul area as quickly as possible. Merchant vessels in the harbor were pressed into evacuation ships while other refugees were sent to Kimpo Airfield in the capital and to a smaller airfield at Suwon, some twenty miles to the south.

From American bases in Japan, the range was extreme for the Lockheed F-80 jets, so yeoman duty fell upon the 68th All-Weather Fighter Squadron based at Itazuke and equipped with North American F-82s. To reinforce these 12 aircraft, part of the 339th All-Weather Fighter Squadron based at Yokota flew its Twin Mustangs to help with the evacuation.

On the morning of June 26, relays of F-82s took up station over Inchon harbor to cover the shipping and truck convoys en route to the port. Initial air action took place at 1333 hours when a Communist fighter dived down and bounced two of the Twin Mustangs. The American pilots were in a quandary as to whether they were authorized to fire back; fortunately the enemy craft didn't decide to mix it up and sped off into the distance.

The following day was a different story. Five Yak fighters came over Kimpo Airfield and were intercepted by five F-82s. In the scrap that followed, the Twin Mustangs scored their only victories of the Korean conflict, as Major James W. Little and Lieutenants William G. Hudson and Charles B. Moran each recorded

F-82s scored the first two aerial victories of the Korean War on June 27, 1940 when Communist aircraft raided Kimpo Airfield. (USAF)

a kill. Later interrogation would bear out the fact that Lieutenant Hudson of the 68th All Weather Fighter Squadron was the first air victor in Korea.

The F-51 Mustangs got into action on the 29th. General MacArthur flew to Suwon to get a firsthand view of the fighting, and a flight of F-51s from Itazuke Air Base in Japan was pressed into service to assist in the aerial cover during the conference. As expected, Yak fighters showed up to strafe the aircraft on the field. The Mustangs entered battle with the four Yaks and tapped all of them in a swift, sharp fight. Lieutenant Orrin Fox was credited with two kills.

Contrary to these initial victories, Korea was not to be a war of aerial conflict for the Mustangs. Shortly after the initial action of the F-82s, they were tied down to defense duties in Japan. Those American, Australian and later the South African F-51 units which saw combat were committed to ground-support action. Particularly while the North Korean offensive rolled south, Mustangs were called on to carry the brunt of air-support missions, for the jets just didn't have the range to permit enough loiter time over the targets. Another North American product, the T-6 ''Texan'' trainer, was called on for duty as liaison aircraft between the ground forces and the fighters. The spotting and targeting achievement of these ''Mosquito'' pilots, as they came to be known, would become legend.

Number 77 RAAF Squadron entered the war on the morning of July 2, 1950 when four Mustangs flew an early morning mission to escort American C-47s bringing wounded out of Korea. The rendezvous was reached successfully and the fighters continued to orbit for several minutes, but the transports never appeared.

South Africa's Number 2 Squadron flew F-51s in Korea. This rocket- and napalm-armed Mustang taxied out for a mission in February 1951. (USAF)

Disappointed and disgruntled, the Australian pilots returned to their base at Iwakuni, Japan. Later in the day they participated in two bomber-escort missions over Korea.

The month of July saw the South Koreans and one American division continue to reel before the onslaught of the Communists from the north. American reinforcements were rushed in from Japan, but months of occupation duty showed its effect in their lack of combat readiness. However, the North Koreans had failed in one respect; their little piston-driven air force was no match for the Americans. Jets and Mustangs of the U. S. Air Force swept them from the skies and strafed their remaining aircraft in the first few days of warfare. There was no air cover for their troops and they suffered accordingly.

Typical of the ground-support missions flown in those trying days was a strike flown on July 14 by No. 77 RAAF Squadron. Four Mustangs contacted the spotter aircraft and were instructed to attack a bridge across the Kum River near Kongju. They hit the bridge with rockets, then they pulled back up to seek targets of opportunity. As they orbited, they were called back to the river to attack enemy troops who were making a crossing in boats.

The Mustangs roared across the scene, skimming the earth with machine guns blazing. The Koreans, caught in the open, were cut down like wheat. A number

A shark-toothed F-51D of the 12th Fighter-Bomber Squadron is pre-flighted for an early-morning mission. (Howard)

of the troops were caught on one side of the river where they waited to cross. Tenaciously they hugged the ground while their comrades were shot down, and, in all probability, they would have been considered dead and left lying had they not jumped up and run when the Mustangs came in for another pass. As it was, many were killed as they scattered in all directions. Then the Mustangs returned and finished off the troops swimming in the river. It was a real massacre.

In order to build up ground-strafing forces, the United States rushed the aircraft carrier USS *Boxer* to Japan with a load of 145 F-51s. She made the crossing in a record-breaking eight days, and the planes were quickly assembled and flown out to combat units.

One of the units so equipped was the 18th Fighter-Bomber Wing which gave up its F-80 jets for Mustangs. This required complete transition and ground-support training, which was conducted on a crash basis. By August they were operating their F-51s in support of the Allied ground forces.

On August 5, 1950, Major Louis J. Sebille took off on a mission with the 67th Squadron of the 18th Fighter-Bomber Wing against enemy artillery and troops hidden along the banks of a river near Hamchang. Flying his wing was Captain Charles R. Morehouse, who was on his first combat mission over Korea, flying

Mustangs of the 18th Fighter-Bomber Wing prepare for a close air support mission in October 1951. Their armament includes HVAR rockets and 500-pound bombs. (USAF)

a Mustang loaded with two 500-pound bombs, six rockets and a full load of .50 caliber ammunition. In the initial bombing attack, Sebille was unable to get rid of one of his bombs, so he racked the plane around and headed back in to make a strafing pass with his flight.

Antiaircraft and small-arms fire was coming up fast and furious that day. Morehouse said later, "They didn't know that they couldn't get away with moving in the daytime and consequently had everything out to throw at us."

Morehouse's radio contact was garbled. He couldnd't make out what his flight leader was saying, but he did hear his element leader, Sebille say, "I'm hit. I'll never make it back. I'm going to get those . . ."

Morehouse followed his leader down on a straight-in strafing run. Sebille was diving for two half-tracks practically hidden in the trees. Morehouse saw the crash, a sheet of flame and the wreckage strewn over the countryside. Major Louis Sebille knew that he had been wounded — probably mortally — and had chosen to dive his stricken aircraft into the midst of the enemy. For this act of final, selfless devotion to duty Major Sebille was awarded the Medal of Honor. It would be the last such award for a gallant Mustang pilot.

The ground-support job by the Mustangs in those days of doubt and anguish was tremendous. By late August, United Nations troops were strong enough to counterattack and retake some of the ground which they had relinquished. At that time ground troops got a firsthand knowledge of the wrath that had been wrought by the F-51s. In the Kigye area, South Korean troops counted over 600 enemy soldiers who had been killed by air strikes, and a few days later over 700 bodies were found in the Pohang area which had been worked over by Mustang bombs and rockets.

Once the United Nations offensive got into gear it was the North Korean Army that retreated under the blows of onrushing round troops which, in this case, were ably supported in the air. By fall of 1950, the enemy had been pushed back far beyond his borders and was reeling toward the Yalu River. It seemed that victory was at hand and there was even talk of American troops going home for Christmas.

United Nations aircraft were overhead everywhere and enemy troops fled in terror. Mustang pilots of the 18th Fighter-Bomber Wing were perhaps the first ever to take prisoners from the air. On this particular occasion two pilots lined up 12 enemy soldiers and marched them four miles to friendly forces by buzzing over their heads.

F-51s operated in the skies over Korea with seeming immunity until they began to strike the enemy in the vicinity of the Yalu River. On November 7, Mustangs were intercepted by MiG-15 jets on five different occasions. In view of the superior performance of this craft, all the F-51 pilot could do was turn inside of him, hit the deck and run for home. But Mustangs remained masters of their prop-driven rivals. The 67th Squadron downed five Yaks in the first six days of November and the 12th Squadron added another.

On November 26 the Chinese Communists entered the war with a full-scale offensive. The suddenness and forcefulness of the attack caught the United Nations troops off balance and once more it was a case of fight and retreat. In foul and freezing weather, the Mustang pilots doggedly flew ground-support missions to cover the escaping infantrymen. On the 28th of December, Mustangs of the 18th FBW bombed and strafed Chinese troops only 80 yards beyond the lines with such intensity that over 100 of the soldiers surrendered.

Some strange and even amusing incidents occurred during the many strafing attacks of the F-51s in Korea. A couple of incidents experienced by pilots of the 18th FBW are related here.

One Mustang pilot passed a field full of haystacks. When he returned, the haystacks had moved to another field. He went down to check them and started to fly on but suddenly the stacks began to move. They were camouflaged Red tanks. They didn't move any more after that — they burned!

Another day two pilots fresh out of rockets and napalm saw a Red tank next to a haystack. They set the haystack afire with .50 caliber maching-gun fire and then fanned the blaze with their prop wash until the tank caught fire and exploded.

On the 19th of January the Australian Mustangs flew an outstanding strike on the Chinese headquarters at Pyongyang. Number 77 Squadron was then attached

This Mustang has been foamed down by crash crews after a Korean belly landing.
(Howard)

to the USAF 35th Fighter Wing for operations at K-9 Airfield out of Pusan, Korea.
USAF Mustangs had tried for two days to get through to the target and had been
turned back by fog, snow and clouds. The Australians were more successful.
Squadron Leader Cresswell led the first two flights of six loaded with bombs. After
the bombs had been dropped the second flight of six would come in with napalm
while the first six used rockets and guns to draw the fire away from them.

Due to weather, the Mustangs got a late start, but at 1300 hours they swept
in and dropped their bombs. Four of them were direct hits and four were near-
misses. One 500-pounder was seen to smash right into the middle of one of the
big brick buildings.

Then the napalm carriers came in, and almost at the same time, USAF B-29s
began to release their bombs over the target. The delay in getting the Mustangs
off that day had overlapped into time for the heavies to make their attack. Undaunted,
the Mustangs bored right on in and put their napalm down on the target despite
the rain of bombs from above and intense antiaircraft fire from below. It seemed
that the Mustangs would get away unscathed, but then on the rise from the target,
pilot Gordon Harvery called out, ''Dropkick Easy One, this engine is losing power.''

He managed to put his plane down on the ice and snow on an island several miles from Pyongyang, but rescue efforts were in vain. He became a prisoner of war.

One of the last victories scored by a Mustang pilot took place on February 5, 1951 when a Yak propeller-driven fighter tried to break up a strafing attack. Major Arnold J. Mullins was heading a flight of three Mustangs. "I was just pulling up from a strafing run when I spotted this Yak directly above me. I let loose with a few bursts from my .50 calibers and scored hits on the cockpit and fuselage. The pilot must have been dead because the plane made a sloppy turn and just kept going. When he crashed, it looked like two napalm bombs exploding."

The Mustangs of the 18th FBW took part in an exceptional bombing and strafing mission against Sinuiju airfield on May 9, 1951. In a bold effort the Reds had built new fuel, supply and ammo dumps at the base and had moved in with 38 Yak-9s, IL-10s and LA-5s. The Fifth Air Force in conjunction with the First Marine Air Wing received the job of knocking it out.

Relays of Sabrejets, Thunderjets and Marine Pantherjets took turns in flying top cover and dispersed the dozen or so MiG-15s which crossed the Yalu to challenge the strike. Waves of Lockheed F-80s went down and suppressed flak with bombs and rockets while Marine Corsairs and Mustangs of the 18th FBW went to work on the dumps and aircraft. Flashing back and forth, dropping bombs, firing rockets and machine guns, the prop-driven planes worked the field over thoroughly. When the American fighters left the scene, all the Red aircraft were destroyed, a large fuel dump was blazing and extensive damage had been inflicted to every other target on the field.

The last aerial scoring for the F-51 took place on the morning of June 20, 1951, when pilots of the 18th FBW fought six Yak-9 fighters over Sinmi Do. Lieutenant J. G. Harrison got one of them with a fine deflection shot. "Them Yaks are flown by a bunch of yaks and there ain't not sweat," was all that the F-51 pilot had to say about the melee. Later that day a Mustang fell to the guns of a MiG-15, but it was one of the few to do so.

Seperate encounters with the MiGs took place on June 20 and 28, but in both cases the F-51s were able to outmaneuver the MiGs and come home, hedgehopping over the treetops.

Tired, obsolete and weary, Mustangs continued to take the war to the Reds on up into 1953. The 18th Wing flew them until January of that year, and Korean pilots performed yeoman duty in them up to the end of hostilities. This time there was no triumph in a burst of glory. It was not the queen of aerial battle that it had been in World War II. This title had passed on from the Mustang to its younger sister from North American, the F-86 Sabrejet. But then, the Mustang could be

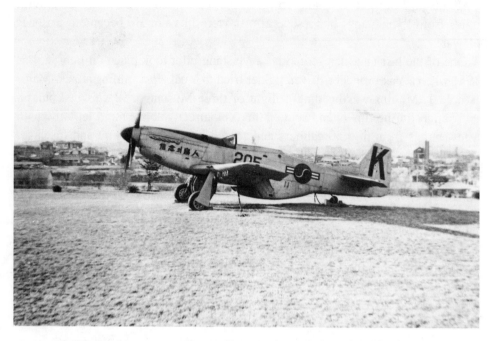

A South Korean Mustang displayed in Seoul after the war. (Doerr)

very, very proud. As a ground-support craft it had done all that could have been asked of it. It may not have been the triumphant chariot that an aspiring ace may have wanted, but ask the infantryman of Korea about the Mustang. He will always remember it. A lot of Communists didn't live to relate the memory.

CHAPTER 12

THE MUSTANG TO DATE

With the end of hostilities in Korea, it seemed the end of the road was near for the Mustang. Most of the P-51Ds and Ks had been used so extensively in that conflict that they were declared "war weary." The South Korean Air Force took the best of the crop remaining in the theater and continued fo fly them for some years.

A rare photo of a US Army F-51D used as a chase plane at Edwards AFB in 1968. (Merryman)

A few National Guard units in the United States were equipped with Mustangs in the middle 1950s, but all of these were gradually replaced by jets. On January 27, 1957 Major James L. Miller, operations officer of the 167th Fighter-Interceptor Squadron of the West Virginia Air National Guard, delivered the last active-duty Mustang to the Air Force Museum at Wright-Patterson AFB, Ohio.

He was met in the air over Patterson Field by Major M. E. Nelson, flying a North American F-100. The scrappy little Mustang and the Super Sabre made several passes over the field for the benefit of photographers, and then on the last fly-by, Major Miller pushed the throttle wide open on the F-51 as did Major Nelson. Of course, the F-100 zoomed up and away from the Mustang in a demonstration of jet power.

The Mustang made one more flight when it was ordered to fly over Marietta, Ohio on February 14, 1957, to celebrate the premiere of the movie *Battle Hymn*, which featured Colonel Dean Hess's career. USAF F-51D, serial number 44-74936 then returned to Wright-Patterson AFB to become a museum piece.

About this same time, Mr. David Lindsay, Jr. formed Trans-Florida Aviation in the city of Sarasota, Florida. Lindsay had been an artillery officer in World War II, but had been impressed by the first P-51 he saw in 1944. He purchased his first Mustang on the surplus market in Canada and taught himself to fly it.

When the Air Force wrote the Mustang completely off its books, Lindsay purchased nearly a hundred, plus spare parts and crated Packard-built Rolls-Royce engines for them. For the next ten years his firm rebuilt quite a number of these aircraft as plush, two-place executive transports for businessmen and sportsmen who wanted to get places in a hurry.

These sleek ex-fighter planes were sold for less than $40,000 plus the cost of avionics and other optional equipment. This so-called Cavalier version of the Mustang was to gain sufficient attention that in due time, Trans-Florida Aviation would adopt the name, Cavalier Aircraft Corporation.

Among the Mustangs that Cavalier has rebuilt and modified is the famous yellow F-51D N2251D which was sold to the parent company, North American. This aircraft, flown by the fabulous aerobatic pilot, Bob Hoover, is a familiar sight at air shows and air races over the nation. One of his most appreciative audiences was the American Fighter Aces Association for whom he performed several years ago. An ex-combat fighter pilot himself, Hoover thrilled them with his spectacular antics. One top-scoring ace was heard to say, "If I had been able to fly a Mustang like that, boy, what a score I could have run up!"

Other than the brilliantly painted Cavaliers which were occasionally seen in and out of major airports, the public saw little and heard little of the Mustang until big-bore racing was revived in 1964. Transcontinental racing as well as pylon racing

Cavalier Aircraft's civilian model in the background and the proposed Military Assistance Program Mustang I in the foreground. Both were modified F-51Ds with improved avionics and H-model tails. (Cavalier)

has made a comeback, but it seems that the latter attracts the most attention these days.

Racing has brought a new generation of pilots to the forefront of their fields and excellent performances are turned in while flying their World War II vintage aircraft. Of course, with new fuels, additives and material for modification that have come to light, they are able to get more out of their Mustangs than some of the early postwar pilots could have dreamed of.

With their souped-up engines, burning 145-octane fuel and using anti-detonation injection, men like Chuck Lyford, Ed Weiner and Chuck Hall really blaze around the pylons, pulling over 100 inches of mercury at times. In recent races Mustangs have averaged better than 400 miles per hour for ten-and twelve-lap pylon races. Pulling those "Gs" around the course and streaking down the straightaways, the Mustang still manages to give a good account of itself.

Much work and ingenuity go into modifying the modern-day racing Mustang. Most of the craft have the wings clipped up to four feet and have fiberglass tips.

The beautifully-painted red, white and blue Mustang formerly operated by the National Aeronautics Association. (Merryman)

Stabilizers have been shortened, and modified propellers and canopies have been installed. Engines are modified to give the greatest possible power for just a short time. This calls for real mechanical engineering and testing right up until racetime. With the margin worked so close for performance, it's not odd that a number of pilots have had their engines blow up on them during a race.

Bob Hoover is often the starter at the big-bore races. He directs the fighters into starting formation and flies right with them to the starters' point. Then Bob gets overhead and monitors the race. Several tragic accidents have been prevented by his timely commentary and advice to the pilots down below.

If an emergency does occur during the race, all pilots pull up to 500 feet and give the aircraft in trouble the complete right-of-way. This gives the man in trouble plenty of room to come in dead stick. Then the racers are cleared to drop back down to low altitude and resume their four to five "G" loads around the pylons.

For safety's sake the majority of air racing is now done in Reno or Las Vegas, Nevada, where good airfields are available and there is not a housing congestion below. Through the efforts of these fine pilots and the interest of the public, it would appear that some of the Mustangs are still going to be around on the racing circuit for some years to come.

In 1967, Cavalier Aircraft Corporation received an order for 12 rebuilt Mustangs from the U. S. Air Force. The planes were not slated for the United States, but for the Military Assistance Program. The first of these fighter planes to go to Central America for counter-insurgency work bore full camouflage paint and were as shiny new as the first P-51A that ever headed for combat duty.

Most of the Mustangs being turned out are single-seat fighters, but some of them are two seated to carry an observer. A few models have been turned out with dual controls for training purposes.

The basic fighter plane uses the old standard wings and fuselage, but has a higher vertical stabilizer as did the P-51H. While basic armament consists of the regular six .50 caliber machine guns, the wings have been strengthened and there are four hardpoints under each wing. The inboard hardpoints can carry either a 110-gallon drop tank or one 1000-pound bomb. The other points are designed to carry five-inch rockets.

In late 1967, Cavalier introduced the Mustang II which principally still has the same features as the original Mustang. However, the Mustang II has further

The only flying B model in the world, as seen in 1984, flown by Pete Regina of Los Angeles. It displayed the markings of Don Gentile's famous "Shangri-La." (Champlin Museum)

Another well-known Mustang on the warbird circuit is Bill Hane's "Ho Hun!" It is based full-time at the Champlin Fighter Museum in Mesa, Arizona. (Hane)

strengthened wings and fuselage, and provides six hardpoints under each wing for ordnance load. Permanent centerline fuel tanks are mounted on the tips of each wing and each will carry 110 gallons of fuel.

With full ordnance load and fuel load, the Mustang II in this new onfiguration has an endurance of seven and a half hours, which would give it an excellent on-station time for counterinsurgency work. Instead of the old V-1650 engine, a 1760 horsepower Merlin 620 is used which increases the gross load capability by some 1200 pounds.

The last model from Cavalier was the Mustang III, which incorporated a Rolls-Royce Dart turboprop engine, giving the plane a maximum dash speed over the target of approximately 470 knots. Standard armament was six .50 caliber machine guns with provision for six minigun pods to be mounted under the wings. Provision was also made to carry 110-gallon drop tanks on the two inboard-wing stations for extended range and loiter time.

It is estimated that there are at least 100 Mustangs flying under civilian registration in the United States in 1985. These, coupled with the Mustangs that Cavalier turned

The world's fastest piston-powered, single-engine aircraft is "Dago Red," operated by Frank Taylor Racing of Chino, California. Built in 1982, it won the Unlimited Class championship at Reno in its first race and in July 1983 established a world record of 517 mph on the 25-kilometer course.

out, assure us that many years will pass before one has to go to a museum to see the sleek-lined aircraft. And as long as old fighter pilots gather to put in a little hangar flying time, there are many, many of them who will attest to the fact that "the Mustang was the best fighter plane that ever flew."

APPENDIX

FLYING EVALUATION OF P-51 B AND D

(As given by Lieutenant Colonel Richard E. Turner, member of the 354th Fighter Group, 356th Fighter Squadron, which was the first operational fighter unit of WW II to fly the Mustang in combat. Colonel Turner flew 109 missions for a total of 309 combat hours in the P-51 and is offically credited with eleven aerial victories and two V-1s. See his memoir; *Big Friend, Little Friend* also from Champlin Press.)

I quote a phrase often used by pilots of the Mustang as the most apt comment I know of which demonstrates the true feeling of practically every pilot who had the good fortune to gain proficiency in flying the P-51. This phrase was, "She's as honest as the day is long and she hasn't a mean bone in her beautiful body!"

The wide landing gear span made takeoff and landing a pleasure to perform and the stall characteristics were straightaway, with an ample warning nibble at the stick to tell the pilot, well in advance, of the imminent drop of the left wing as torque snatched at the completely stalled aircraft. Even after experiencing the dropping left wing, one could regain flying control by applying full throttle and co-ordinating right rudder.

Rudder control during taxi operations on the ground was positive, due to a mechanical linkage hookup between the rudder action and the tail wheel when the stick was held to the rear of center position, thus enabling the pilot to steer the aircraft into gradual turns without using the brakes. During ground operation it was SOP [standard operating procedure] to place the coolant flaps in the manual full-open position, returning them to automatic-control operation in the pretakeoff check. Thereafter, the heat requirements of the engine automatically adjusted the coolant flaps.

As a rule, I kept my fighter trimmed for combat-cruise conditions since the majority of my flight time was under these circumstances. Normally, the only major departure from this trim configuration occurred when I found myself under prolonged instrument conditions, at which time I could trim for the speed and conditions at hand. I found that this practice relieved me from some of the physical strain generated on instruments, and therefore helped reduce somewhat the rate of build-up of mental tension inevitably acquired while endeavoring to penetrate a frontal system, or letting down through huge weather build-ups over home-base area after returning from a combat mission over the Continent. Although the Mustang flew well under instrument conditions, due in my opinion to the light control feel and quick response to any maneuver, I was never loath to grab a free letdown by latching onto a handy bomber formation when I could find one in my vicinity. The bomber boys didn't seem to mind my hitch-hiking tendencies on instruments; in fact several times the bomber that I glued onto would flip on his running lights to help me keep visual contact in the thick weather. It was rather like a case of "You scratch my back and I'll scratch yours." Actually, the instrument flying didn't bother me as much as the thought of letting down in the soup amid all the hundreds of other bombers and fighters that had to be doing the same thing in a mad, crazy-quilt pattern of descending aircraft. Tucked into the middle of a nice bunch of B-17s gave me the comforting feeling of having a solid barrier between me and other aircraft in my particular bit of sky.

The general flight characteristics of the Mustang were all that a pilot could ask, especially the original P-51B. As a matter of fact, I felt that the P-51 made most pilots look much better than their level of skill should allow them to appear. It took a pretty heavy-handed man with a proclivity toward mental lapse in order to actually look bad as a pilot in a Mustang, for the sleek little fighter had a most forgiving nature. In comparison with other fighters in combat of its era, such as the P-47, P-38, P-40, Me-109 and FW-190, the Mustang performed favorably in practically every category.

Two features of the Mustang's engine which pilots particularly enjoyed consisted of the supercharger and fuel-mixture-control arrangement. They were both actuated and controlled by a barometric switch. In the case of the supercharger, your crew chief could preset the altitude at which you wanted the extra boost to cut in and the barometric switch automatically cut in at that altitude without further bother to the pilot. We set ours for 14,000 feet cut-in, and there was no doubt in the pilot's mind as to when it cut in, for he felt a definite surge of new power which provided him with a kick in the tail to remind him that he had new horses to chase the enemy. The mixture control when in the auto position likewise had a barometric sensing switch which maintained the correct mixture according to the altitude of the aircraft, and in the heat of combat the less a pilot had to dwell on the operation requirements of his equipment, the better he can concentrate on the tactical problems at hand which could in almost every combat engagement mean the difference between success and disaster.

According to the specifications, the Mustang was supposed to be able to deliver a maximum speed of 395 mph at 5000 feet, but from my personal experience I know this to be a low figure, for I attained maximum speeds of 450 mph straight and level while chasing and catching the notorious ''Buzz-bomb,'' or V-1s as the Germans called them. As far as comparable fighter speeds are concerned, I have only the combat fighters pilot's measuring stick to go by. I remember clearly that I was able to close and catch any bogey within reasonable range that I chased with determination, and due to the ample confidence instilled in me via my faith in the Mustang's capability to take all comers, I did not participate in any engagement with the enemy without feelings an underlying conviction that I was the hunter and not the hunted.

One of the many factors which fostered and bolstered this feeling was the excellent maneuvering ability, radius of turn and rate of roll. The P-51 could keep up with any aircraft and surpass most in this department so dear to a fighter pilot's heart. The P-51B was a veritable dream come true for a pilot in this department. It was the first aircraft that I had ever flown that I could pull up from cruising power to execute a perfect loop without adding power; to me this added up to a near-perfect wedding of power-to-weight ratio which gave the Mustang its nimbleness in maneuver and delicate but good feel through the control stick.

As usual, when the engineers tried improving the original model with modifications and added features, they increased the weight without a commmensurate increase in power; so when the P-51D came out later, it lacked some of the delicate balance and aerobatic capabilities. But with its improved visibility and still good performance, compared to the enemy equipment, it was still a winner. After I flew it a short while I enjoyed and believed in it as much as I had the ''B'' model.

One of the few disadvantages found in the P-51B was the greenhouse-type canopy on the production model which severly restricted visibility, especially to the rear, but his was soon remedied by the availability of an English modification known as the Malcolm hood. This modification gave the best visibility that I was ever to enjoy from the cockpit of a fighter. I could actually lean out of the cockpit and look under and behind my own fighter's tail a very comforting bit of insurance to have available during a large helter-skelter mixed-up dogfight. The P-51D which followed had a one-piece plastic canopy that approached this visibility, but which did not quite equal it.

An operational bug which developed and gave us temporary trouble was the four .50 caliber machine guns. They were mounted on an angle canted to the inboard around thirty degrees instead of upright, due to the thin profile of the laminar-flow wing design. This angle-off mounting caused a binding effect to be exerted on the ammo belts during turns of any appreciable G-force which in turn tended to cause at least three of the guns to jam. Since the pilot had no clearing mechanism, and G-force was almost synonymonus with combat for fighters this problem gave us great concern at first. The only recourse a pilot had, since one firing gun usually rendered using the gunsight useless, was to ride the rudders and spray the bullets from the operable gun like a hose, hoping for a lucky hit. Again, this deficiency was corrected in short order by a modificatition figured out and installed by our own ingenious and hard-working ground crewmen. They liberated some ammo-booster motors from a B-26 group nearby and rigged them on our fighter's ammo belts which, for all practical purposes, eliminated all such stoppages in the future. In the later model P-51D there were six guns, but all were mounted upright, effectively solving the former problem.

While engaging enemy aircraft in aerial combat, I found the P-51B and D equal to all demands and maneuvering requirements that I asked of it. The only area of flying under combat conditions that I consciously avoided was that of a low speed, which I felt robbed my Mustang of its intrinsic design advantages. In normal combat speeds between 300 and 420 mph, the controls retained good feel and flexibility which subconsciously prompted good natural co-ordination and flying skill from the pilot while he concentrated wholly upon the tactical situation or requirement at hand. Even in extreme high speeds attained in vertical dives while chasing a fleeing enemy aircraft, the Mustang was manageable for the pilot who maintained his composure and was responsive to the message relayed through the feel of the controls. From 500 mph through 650 mph in a protracted vertical dive, the controls stiffened appreciably and tended to slip quickly into compression stalls upon direct-manual effort to pull out of the dive by exerting back pressure on the control column. This clumsy manual effort during a high-speed pullout was about the only maneuver where pilot error could materially affect a design overload which could cause airframe damage or destruction in the case of a ham-fisted insensitive pilot. I went through several of these very high-speed dives, and actually experienced compressibility buffeting from a speed which I assume was in excess of the design limit, since I was going straight down at the time, with the airspeed needle quivering against the peg, past 650 mph. This was before even attempting a pullout. In every instance I effected a controlled pullout by initiating recovery procedure through rudder-tab-control action until the aircraft flew through the critical bottom-out portion of the recovery, at which time normal manual-control characteristics returned almost immediately.

Up until the Mustang arrived on the combat scene in the ETO in November 1943, the favorite effective evasive maneuver of the Me-109s was to roll over on their backs and split-ess in a vertical dive for the deck, relying on their quick-diving acceleration speed to extricate them from trouble. The Mustang blew this evasive tactic into the halls of hades. With Mustangs around, the Me-109 pilot could hardly get his plane into the vertical position before he found a couple of

P-51s closing into deadly range behind him. From 30,000 feet I could spot an Me-109 a 5000-foot head start in a dive and catch him before he passed 15,000 feet. We considered diving enemy aircraft as easy meat.

High-altitude performance of the Mustang left little to be desired when compared to the capabilities of the enemy. To demonstrate this point I recall one particular escort mission on April 8, 1944, during which we escorted B-17s. The big friends were flying inbound around 25,000 feet, approaching their IP [initial point] deep inside Germany, and our group had its Mustangs deployed around the bomber stream to intercept any enemy fighter thrusts at the bombers. I had two flights of my 356th Fighter Squadron at 27,000 feet just over the bomber stream, on station as high cover. We had been flying our sector patrol for about fifteen minutes after rendezvous when I discovered very high contrails approaching the bomber stream from the interior at extremely high altitude. I was slightly startled at the apparent altitude of the bogies, which I judged to be around 40,000 feet. i disengaged my own Red Flight from area patrol, leaving the other flight to mind the store, and commenced climbing to intercept the contrails which had to be enemy fighters, considering the unfriendly direction from which they were coming.

After 10 to 15 minutes of maximum climbing, we found ourselves converging on a collision course with 20 Me-109s. We had no choice in giving the enemy a height advantage as we closed from below, but I considered this compensated for by the fact we had them in sight and lined up for instant attack-position pass, if needed, from the start of our intercepting climb. As we were closing into approximate firing range, I noticed the altimeter needle nibbling at 40,000 feet on the dial, but I still had a positive feel and control response with no apparent mushiness or lag time. I picked out the nearest enemy fighter with my gun-sight pip as the German formation tried to roll into us for a pass. Instead, almost as if on cue, the whole gaggle of enemy planes stalled and snap-rolled into a gyrating mass of uncontrollable spins in the rarefied air. I saw at least one mid-air collision between three or four Me-109s as the stricken and floundering mass of fighters dropped helplessly below us.

Instantly, on instinct I rolled my own flight into an attack on the mass of milling German fighters presented to us by virtue of the mass error committed before our guns. Those beautiful little Mustangs answered their controls without protest of any sort, and we were able to make three deadly passes through the frantic melee of struggling Germans, scoring from four to six kills before they could recover control. It was an awesome but confidence-building experience for us and exposed depths of capability in our Mustangs that we hadn't realized they possessed.

Our Mustangs were the first long-range fighters in the ETO capable of penetrating enemy territory as deeply as the heavy bombers, and although we were assigned administratively to the Ninth Air Force, we were flying operationally under the

Eighth Air Force. This unique arrangement was fostered by the fact that we were the only fighters available that could provide escort over targets deep inside Germany as well as penetration and withdrawal. We didn't mind or object to this arrangement because we were afforded ample opportunity to engage and destroy enemy fighters which is the ultimate reward to a fighter pilot. But some months before D-day of the invasion of the Continent, we found our usual heavy-escort missions being interspersed between new tactical support-type missions such as dive bombing, area interdiction strafing and armed reconnaissance which required a superior low-altitude performance from our aircraft. Once again the Mustang displayed an excellent degree of adaptability and a capability to execute the critical maneuvering close to the ground required to successfully carry out these new-type missions. Here again, the P-51B and D by virtue of their maneuvering nimbleness brought new enthusiasm, verve and style to tactical support work.

I agree that the sturdy, indefatigable work horse, the P-47, on the face of it, was less vulnerable to ground fire with its huge air-cooled power plant, but at the same time it was much larger and less maneuverable at low altitude. The Mustang on the other hand was a smaller target, requiring less maneuvering room and could get in and out quicker on a strike with better visual coverage. At any rate, all ground tactical targets which possessed any appreciable concentration of ground-defense firepower was more or less like playing Russian roulette to a fighter pilot. He assumed the fatalist's attitude of throw the dice and take your chances! The opportunity and excitement of firing on a target was more than enough to enable the confirmed fighter pilot to forget or dismiss the unfavorable odds attributed to low-level work.

In summation, the inevitable conclusion concerning the P-51B and D Mustang fighter of World War II has to be that it is acknowledged as the best all-around fighter aircraft of its era. With pilotage being equal, it could match the performance of any competitor, friend or foe, and more often than not come up with that something extra in performance that enabled it to emerge as top dog in any fight. As dramatic proof of this contention that I can vouch for from personal knowledge, my squadron, the 356th Fighter Squadron of the 354th Fighter Group, flew approximately 18 months of continuous combat operations during which it participated in every known type of mission. As a result the squadron destroyed over 200 enemy aircraft in the air and lost only 22 pilots as fatal casualties from all causes, training accidents as well as combat losses. This unusual record of kills versus losses was made possible, for the most part, due to the intrinsic advangage afforded us by the superior capabilities of our aircraft, the P-51B and P-51D Mustangs.

TABLE OF MUSTANG VITAL STATISTICS

Model	Engine	Top Speed MPH	Wing Span	Length	Loaded Weight Lbs.	Quan.	Remarks
NA-73X	1100 h.p.-Allison V-1710-39	—	37'	32'3"	7965	1	Original prototype
Mustang I	1100 h.p.-Allison V-1710-39	380	37'	32'3"	8606	320	To Royal Air Force. 4 — .30-cal. & 4 — .50-cal. machine guns. Serials AG 345/664.
XP-51	1100 h.p.-Allison V-1710-39	380	37'	32'3"	8606	(2)	4th and 10th Mustang Is production models to USAAC Serial AC 41-38 & 39.
Mustang I	1100 h.p.-Allison V-1710-39	382	37'	32'3"	8625	300	Forward coolant scoop redesigned. Serials AL 958/999. Am 100/257. AP 164/263.
P-51	1100 h.p.-Allison V-1710-39	387	37'	32'3"	8800	148	Originally ordered by Royal Air Force. Armed w/4 — 20-mm cannon. 93 to Royal Air Force as Mustang IAs and 55 to USAAF as F-6As w/K-24 cameras.
P-51A	1200 h.p.-Allison V-1710-81	390	37'	32'3"	9000	310	Engine change. 4 — .50-cal. machine guns. 50 to Royal Air Force as Mustang II.
XP-51B	1360 h.p.-Packard V-1650-3	441	37'	32'3"	8430	(2)	P-51 w/engine change. 1st designated XP-78. Serial 41-37352 & 41-37421.
A-36	1325 h.p.-Allison V-1710-87	356	37'	32'3"	10,000	500	P-51 w/dive flaps and wing racks. Serials 42-83663 to 42-84162.

Model	Engine	Top Speed MPH	Wing Span	Length	Loaded Weight Lbs.	Quan.	Remarks
P-51B-10-NA	1360 h.p.-Packard V-1650-3	436	37'	32'3"	11,800	1598	Production model w/Packard-built Merlin engine. 4 — .50-cal. machine guns. Serials 42-106429/738, 43-6313/7202, 43-12093/492. 274 P-51Bs to Royal Air Force as Mustang III. 71 P-51Bs modified to F-6C-NA.
P-51B-15-NA	1450 h.p.-Packard V-1650-7	439	37'	32'3"	11,800	390	Engine change. Serials 43-24752/901, 42-106739/978.
P-51C-1-3-NT	1360 h.p.-Packard V-1650-3	436	37'	32'3"	11,800	350	P-51B built in Dallas.
P-51C-10-NT	1450 h.p.-Packard V-1650-7	439	37'	32'3"	11,800	1400	Dallas-built P-51Bs w/engine change. Serials 42-103329/978, 43-24902/25251. 44-10753/11152. 636 P-51Cs to Royal Air Force as Mustang III. 20 P-51Cs modified as F-6C-NT for USAAF.
P-51D-NA	1450 h.p.-Packard V-1650-7	437	37'	32'3"	12,100 (Max.)	6502	Bubble canopy. 6 — .50-cal. machine guns. 281 P-51Ds to Royal Air Force as Mustang IV. 136 P-51Ds modified to F-6D-NA for USAAF. Serials 42-106539/540, 44-13253/15752. 44-63160/64159. 44-72027/75026.
P-51D-NT	1450 h.p.-Packard V-1650-7	437	37'	32'3"	12,100	1454	P-51D built in Dallas. Serials 44-11153/352, 44-84390/989, 45-11343/742.

Model	Engine	Top Speed MPH	Wing Span	Length	Loaded Weight Lbs.	Quan.	Remarks
TP-51D-NT	1450 h.p.-Packard V-1650-7	435	37'	32'3"	11,300	10	Fighter-trainer. Serials 44-84610/611, 45-11443/450.
XP-51F	1450 h.p.-Packard V-1650-7	466	37'	32'3"	9060	3	Lightweight version. 4 — .50-cal. machine guns. Serials 43-43332/34.
XP-51G	1500 h.p.-Rolls-Royce Merlin 145	472	37'	32'3"	8885	2	Engine change and Aero Products prop. Serials 43-43335/36.
P-51H	1380 h.p.-Packard V-1650-9	487	37'	33'4"	11,500	555	Engine change. 2218 h.p. w/water injection. 6 — .50-cal. machine guns. Serials 44-64160/714.
XP-51J	1500 h.p.-Allison V-1710-119	480+	37'	32'1"	9140	2	Engine change. 4 — .50-cal. machine guns. Serials 44-76027/28.
P-51K-NT	1450 h.p.-Packard V-1650-7	437	37'	32'3"	12,100	1337	P-51D made in Dallas with Aero Products prop. 594 to Royal Air Force as Mustang IV. 163 modified to F-6D-NT for USAAF. Serials 44-11353/12852.
P-51M	1400 h.p.-Packard V-1650-9A	491	37'	33'4"	11,500	1	P-51H with engine change. Serial 45-11743.
XP-82	2-1400 h.p.-Packard V-1650-23/25	480	51'3"	38'1"	24,600	2	First Twin Mustangs. Serials 44-83886/887.
XP-82A	2-1500 h.p.-Allison V-1710-119	482	51'3"	38'1"	25,000	1	Engine change. Serial 44-83888.
P-82B	2-1400 h.p.-Packard V-1650-9	482	51'3"	38'1"	24,800	20	Production version of Twin Mustang. Serials 44-65160/179.
P-82C	2-1400 h.p.-Packard V-1650-23	481	51'3"	38'1"	25,000	(1)	10th P-82B for all-weather testing.

Model	Engine	Top Speed MPH	Wing Span	Length	Loaded Weight Lbs.	Quan.	Remarks
P-82D	2-1400 h.p.-Packard V-1650-23	480	51'3"	38'1"	25,000	(1)	P-82B for all-weather testing. Radar pod.
P-82E	2-1600 h.p.-Allison V-1710-143/ 145	478	51'3"	39'	24,900	100	P-82B with engine change. Serials 46-255/354.
P-82F	2-1600 h.p.-Allison V-1710-143/ 145	410	51'3"	39'	26,226	100	P-82E for all-weather fighting. Serials 46-405/504.
P-82G	2-1600 h.p.-Allison V-1710-143/ 145	410	51'3"	39'	26,000	50	With new and larger radar equipment. Serials 46-355/404.

MUSTANG COMBAT UNITS OF WORLD WAR II
U. S. ARMY AIR FORCES

1st Air Commando Group: Operated P-47s and P-51s within its India-based units from February 1944 until May 1944. These P-51s bombed and strafed enemy airdromes and positions in addition to flying escort for bombers and cargo aircraft of the unit. The P-51s flew many sorties covering Wingate's invasion of Burma in March and April of 1944. Markings: Five diagonal stripes around the fuselage, aft of the cockpit.

2nd Air Commando Group: Between November 1944 and May 1945, the Mustangs operating with this unit supported Allied forces by striking enemy airfields and transport from their bases in India. Flew support for cargo aircraft and were used as escort for bombers to targets in the vicinity of Rangoon. Did bombing in Thailand and flew reconnaissance missions.

3rd Air Commando Group: Fifth Air Force. Went into action in the Philippines in late 1944. Its Mustangs flew ground support and attacked enemy installations, particularly on Luzon. Escorted bombers to Formosa and the China coast. Made numerous fighter sweeps against airfields and rail targets on Formosa.

4th Fighter Group: Eighth Air Force. This unit, which was composed of the old Eagle Squadrons, got its Mustangs in February 1944 and flew its first combat mission in them on the 25th. Flew many outstanding bombers-escort missions. On March 3, 1944, two flights of Mustangs routed more than 60 Luftwaffe fighters in the Berlin area, destroying six of them. The effect of the new Mustangs showed immediately. The unit destroyed 156 e/a in March 1944. On a mission to Brunswick on April 8, 1944, the P-51s shot down 31 Germans for the loss of four Mustangs. Led first shuttle mission from England to Russia on June 21, 1944. Completed many very successful strafing missions against German airfields in the spring of 1945. Markings: Red spinners and cowling. Sqdn. code letters: 334th-QP, 335th-WD, 336th-VF. Top P-51 ace: Captain D. S. Gentile, 16½ victories.

8th Reconnaissance Group: Used some F-6 Mustangs on photo and reconnaissance missions over Burma, China, French Indochina and Thailand during 1944. Also did some bombing and strafing in addition to bomber-escort duty.

10th Photo Reconnaissance Group: Ninth Air Force. Operated the first P-51A which had been fitted out as camera aircraft in England. Later utilized F-6 aircraft as a portion of the unit's command. These Mustangs did extensive visual- and photo-reconnaissance work until the end of the war in Europe. Sqdn. Code Letters: (There was considerable interchange of squadrons between the recce groups during the war. Listed here are codes of squadrons which flew with both the 10th and 67th Reconnaissance Groups.) 12th Sqdn.-ZM, 15th Sqdn.-5M, 107th Sqdn.-AX, 109th Sqdn.-VX.

15th Fighter Group: VII Fighter Command. Received P-51s in late 1944 and moved to Iwo Jima in February 1945. Supported the ground forces on the island during March 1945. Began strikes against airfields, shipping and installations on the other islands in the Bonins in late March. Flew its first very long range mission escorting the B-29s to Japan on April 7, 1945. The mission met with heavy opposition and the Mustangs of this unit were credited with destroying 17 enemy fighters. Continued to escort the B-29s until they turned to night missions and then flew fighter sweeps over the Japanese home islands until the end of the war. Markings: 45th F.S.-Deep-green diagonal bands with narrow black borders on the wings, horizontal and vertical tail surfaces. Spinner from front was banded black, green and silver. 47th F.S.-Black stripes with narrow yellow bands on the wings, just outboard of the machine guns, on the horizontal tail and about the aft fuselage. On the vertical tail was an iverted black triangle, with narrow yellow bands. Spinner from front was banded yellow, black and yellow. 78th F.S.-Tips of the wings and horizontal and vertical tails painted yellow with a black band, of equal width, inboard or below the yellow. Spinner was painted all yellow and the forward part of the nose was black. Top ace: Captain R. W. Moore, 12 victories.

20th Fighter Group: Eighth Air Force. This unit converted to P-51s on July 17, 1944. Began Mustang operations on July 20 and drew first blood five days after the switchover when Lieutenants Moncrieff and Adams surprised and broke up a formation of 50 Me-109s over central Germany. After destroying three of them, they then attacked another formation of over fifty Me-109s and were able to make a getaway. Had outstanding strafing missions on August 25 and October 6 when 30 and 40 German planes, respectively, were destroyed on the ground. Destroyed 28 German fighters in the air while escorting the bombers to Merseburg on November 2, 1944. Fought off Me-262s while escorting bombers north of Berlin on April 10, 1945. Pilots of the unit credited with five of the jets. Markings: Alternate white and black stripes starting from the spinner and continuing to the aft engine cowling. Sqdn. code letters: 55th-KI, 77th-LC, 79th-MC. Top ace: Captain E. C. Fiebelkorn, 9½ victories.

21st Fighter Group: VII Fighter Command. Moved to Iwo Jima in Mustangs during February-March 1945. Sustained casualties during Japanese banzai charge on the night of March 26-27, but flew first combat mission the next day against airfield on Haha Jima. Won Distinguished Unit Citation for the first VLR escort mission with the B-29s on April 7, 1945. Continued to fly escort missions and, later, primarily fighter sweeps against the Japanese home islands until the end of the war. Markings: A horizontal band on the vertical tail, the wingtips and horizontal tailtips and the spinner being of a squadron color — Blue for the 46th F.S., yellow for the 72nd F.S. and white for the 531st F.S. A narrow black band bordered the color markings, while another was placed behind the spinner. Top Score: Captain H. L. Crim, 6 victories.

23rd Fighter Group: Fourteenth Air Force. The famed "Flying Tiger" Group flew its first P-51 mission on November 23, 1943, when it participated on the mission against the island of Formosa. In that attack, the pilots shot down five enemy fighters in the air and destroyed four on the ground. From December 1943 until April 1944 the group was primarily engaged in fighter sweeps, dive-bombing and strafing missions. The unit received a DUC for its action against Japanese ground forces during June 17-25, 1945, when the enemy launched an all-out attack down the Siang River valley in Hunan Province, China. Despite adverse weather and intense enemy ground fire, the Mustangs of the 23rd destroyed much enemy equipment and shipping and killed over 1600 troops. The group continued to support ground troops by attacking enemy-troop installations and to fly attacks against harbor facilities at Shanghai, Canton and Hong Kong to the end of the war. Top P-51 ace: Lieutenant Colonel J. C. Herbst, 18 victories.

27th Fighter-Bomber Group: Equipped with A-36s in North Africa where it joined the Twelfth Air Force in June of 1943. Flew dive-bombing and strafing missions against Pantelleria and supported ground forces in the invasion and conquest of Sicily. Provided air cover for the invasion of Italy at Salerno and received a DUC for their air attacks against German armored columns on September 10, 1943. Continued to support Fifth Army troops in their A-36s until June 1944 when the unit converted to P-47s. Top Score: Lieutenant M. J. Russo, 5 victories.

31st Fighter Group: Converted from Spitfires to Mustangs when it joined the Fifteenth Air Force in Italy in April 1944. This unit scored 379 aerial victories flying the P-51 between this date and the end of the war. In their first month of Mustang operations the group won a DUC for their performance on April 21. On a mission to Ploesti, Rumania, a weather recall was given, but some of the bombers apparently didn't receive the message and continued to the target. The 31st went on to provide escort and broke up a massive attack of enemy fighters, destroying seventeen of them. The unit received a second DUC for their action during the Russian shuttle mission of 22-26 July 1944. On their second day in Russia they flew a mission over the German-Polish front lines where they encountered a bevy of e/a and destroyed thirty of them in the air and a further thirteen on the ground. During the shuttle mission the 31st shot down thirty-seven enemy aircraft and lost none of their own. The last real ''big'' mission for the unit was the trip to Berlin on March 24, 1945 which saw the 31st tangle with the German Me-262 jets and in the encounter shot five of them from the sky without a loss of their own. Markings: Red spinners and diagonal red and white stripes on the vertical tail. Sqdn. Code Letters: 307th-MX, 308th-HL, 309th-WZ. Top score: Major J. J. Voll, 21 victories.

35th Fighter Group: Fifth Air Force. This veteran unit received P-51s while stationed on Luzon in the Philippine Islands in March of 1945. Flew numerous ground-support operations as well as fighter sweeps and bomber-escort missions to Formosa and China. Moved to Okinawa in June of 1945. Flew several fighter sweeps over Kyushu and missions to Korea and the China coast before V-J Day. 39th, 40th and 41st Fighter Squadrons. Top P-51 score: Captain R. A. Mittlestadt, 3 victories.

51st Fighter Group: The veteran 51st Group came to the Fourteenth Air Force from the Tenth Air Force in October 1943. Its China based squadrons began replacing their Curtis P-40s with P-51B and C Mustangs in March 1944. The Mustangs of the 51st Group flew nemerous missions in support of Chinese ground troops throughout their offensive in the summer and fall of 1944. Despite inclimate weather their P-51s made numerous rail cuts, sunk small enemy river vessels and cut off the enemy's supplies. 1945 saw the 51st striking Japanese installations along the Old Burma Road, and many strikes were flown against targets in French Indo-China. Markings: Most of the early OD-painted Mustangs were adorned with shark's teeth on the noses. Aircraft numbers were painted on either the vertical stabilizer or on the side of the fuselage as follows: 16th FS-350-399; 25th FS-200-249; 26th FS-250-299. Late 1944 Mustangs of the 26th FS utilized yellow bands outlined with black on horizontal and vertical surfaces. 25th FS had black checker-board vertical tails.

52nd Fighter Group: This ex-Spitfire unit received its P-51s in April and May 1944 when it was assigned to the Fifteenth Air Force in Italy. From May until the end of the war, the unit's Mustangs ranged over Germany, Austria, Czechoslovakia and the Balkans to provide escort for the heavy bombers. On June 9, 1944, their Mustangs provided superior escort to a scattered bomber stream attacking targets at Munich, Germany, and broke up successive concentrations of enemy fighters. In the running air battle, 14 German fighters were shot down without the loss of a single P-51. A highly successful strafing mission was flown by the group on August 31, 1944, when they strafed Reghin landing ground in Rumania. Despite aerial opposition and ground flak, the Mustangs of the 52nd managed to wreak havoc by destroying 60 airplanes on the ground while the top cover downed nine of the intercepting aircraft. Markings: Red spinners and yellow aft fuselage and tail surfaces. Top Score: Captain J. S. Varnell, 17 victories.

55th Fighter group: Eighth Air Force. This group converted to Mustangs from P-38s on July 14, 1944. They were not long in displaying their prowess in the new craft as is exemplified by their record between September 3 and 13, 1944. In addition to escorting bombers and breaking up concentrations of enemy fighters they went down and wrecked Luftwaffe airdromes on the way home. During the ten-day period they destroyed 106 enemy aircraft in the air and on the ground. On February 19, 1945, its proficiency as a strafing unit was further demonstrated when the Mustangs went down to the deck to destroy eighty-one locomotives. The following day they broke their own record when they chalked up 89 locomotives. Markings: Spinner from front banded green, yellow and green. Two bands of green-and-yellow checks aft of the spinner. Sqdn. code letters: 38th-CG, 338th-CL, 343rd-CY. Top scorer: Lieutenant W. H. Lewis, 8 victories.

67th Tactical Reconnaissance Group: Ninth Air Force. Operated a number of squadrons at various periods of time that utilized P-51 and F-6 aircraft. Did excellent work on a wide variety of photo recce, visual recce, weather recce and bomb-damage-assessment missions. Mustangs of this unit also took their toll of enemy aircraft when they encountered them in the course of their mission. Four squadrons flew Mustangs with the group at various times. Code letters: 12th-ZM, 15th-SM, 107th-AX, 109th-VX.

68th Tactical Reconnaissance Group: Used some Mustangs for photo- and visual-reconnaissance missions from its bases in Italy. These aircraft ranged over France, Germany, Austria and the Balkans.

69th Tactical Reconnaissance Group: Ninth Air Force. Began operations in F-6s in March 1945. Flew visual- and photo-recce missions up to V-E Day. Sqdn. Code Letters: 10th Sqdn.-YC, 22nd Sqdn.-QL.

71st Tactical Reconnaissance Group: Fifth Air Force. Received some P-51s and F-6s in late 1944. Flew many missions over the Philippines, Formosa and China. Major William Shomo won the Congressional Medal of Honor flying one of its Mustangs on January 11, 1945, when he encountered and shot down seven enemy planes while on a visual-reconnaissance mission. Squadrons: 82nd and 110th TRS.

78th Fighter Group: Last Eighth Air Force fighter group to convert to P-51s. Received its first Mustangs in late December 1944. Its fighters did excellent strafing work in the spring of 1945. On April 10, 1945, they destroyed 52 e/a on an airfield in Czechoslovakia and six days later they went back to another Czech airfield and racked up a record total of 135 planes destroyed and eighty-nine damaged on the ground. Markings: Black-and-white-checkerboard cowling. Sqdn. Code Letters: 82nd-MX, 83rd-HL, 84th-WZ.

86th Fighter-Bomber Group: Twelfth Air Force. Flew many dive-bombing and strafing missions in its A-36s which it received in North Africa in July of 1943. Supported ground forces in Sicily and at Salerno during the invasion of Italy. 525th, 526th and 527th Squadrons.

311th Fighter Group: Tenth Air Force. Began operations in A-36s and P-51s late in 1943. While based in India its Mustangs flew many bomber-escort and ground-support missions. In July 1944 the unit moved to Burma where it gave excellent cover to Allied ground forces. The group moved to China in August 1944 and was used primarily as bomber escort up to the end of the war. 528th, 529th and 530th Squadrons.

325th Fighter Group: Fifteenth Air Force. Received P-51s in May 1944 and was selected as the Mustang group to escort bombers on the first shuttle mission to Russia from Italy on June 2, 1941. The unit scored many aerial victories while flying cover for the heavies, but they also excelled in strafing. On September 8, 1944, they attacked two landing fields in Yugoslavia and of the 106 aircraft parked on the fields only five escaped destruction. One flight from the unit intercepted a force of 48 Luftwaffe fighters attacking the bombers on the afternoon of October 16, 1944, and shot nine of them down. The bombers returned unscathed. Their last big air battle took place on March 14, 1945, when the unit's Mustangs took on 38 FW-190s over Hungary and shot down 17 of them. Markings: Red spinners and black-and-yellow-checkerboard tail surfaces. Top P-51 ace: Captain Harry Parker, 13 victories.

332nd Fighter Group: Fifteenth Air Force. The last fighter group of the Fifteenth AF to receive Mustangs. Began its P-51 operations in June of 1944. Primarily engaged in bomber-escort missions, but also flew some highly successful strafing raids in the Balkans. This all-Negro unit won a DUC when it fought off German jets attacking the bombers on a mission to Berlin on March 24, 1945. Markings: Red spinners and tail surfaces. 99th, 301st and 302nd Fighter Squadrons. Top Scores: Lieutenants L. A. Archer and E. L. Toppins, 4 victories.

339th Fighter Group: Eighth Air Force. This unit arrived in England in March of 1944 and began its operations by flying a sweep in its P-51s on April 30, 1944. On September 11, 1944, its Mustangs attacked 100-plus German fighters which were queuing up to intercept the bombers. In the air battle which followed, fifteen of the enemy were destroyed. The same day, one squadron of the group strafed an airfield near Karlsruhe and destroyed twenty planes on the ground. This unit also flew some very successful Me 262 suppression missions in early 1945, destroying a number of them in the air and many on the ground. In a year of combat, the 339th destroyed 239½ e/a in the air and 440½ e/a on the ground. Markings:

Spinner from the front banded white, red and white. Sqdn. code letters: 503rd.-D7, 504th-6N, 505th-5Q. Top score: Major W. E. Bryan, 8½ victories.

348th Fighter Group: This veteran 5th Air Froce group gave up its P-47s in January 1945 and was equipped with P-51Ds. The 348th continued to support American troops desteroying enemy resistance on Luzon in the Philippines. Hundreds of ground support missions were flown, many utilizing napalm to burn out the entrenched Japanese. Later the group flew its longest escort missions covering strikes by B-25s against enemy shipping in the South China Sea. Markings: Used old pre-World War II horizontal red and white stripes on rudders. Vertical band on the aft fin in squadron color. Aircraft number painted on vertical strips in most cases. Black theater bands painted around aft fuselage.

352nd Fighter Group: Eighth Air Force. Gave up its P-47s for Mustangs on April 7, 1944. On May 8, 1944, intercepted 100-plus enemy fighters attacking the bomber stream in the vicinity of Bremen. Shot down twenty-seven planes in the air battle that ranged from 23,000 feet to the deck. Shot down thirty-eight e/a attacking the bombers in the Dresden area on November 2, 1944. 487th Squadron downed twenty-three e/a attacking their airdrome at Asch, Belgium, on New Year's Day 1945. Markings: Blue spinners and cowling. Sqdn. code letters: 328th-PE, 486th-PZ, 487th-HO. Top P-51 ace: Major G. E. Preddy, 23.83 victories.

353rd Fighter Group: Eighth Air Force. Converted from P-47s to P-51s on September 30, 1944. Gave invaluable support to the bombers on missions deep into Germany, and destroyed many enemy aircraft on strafing missions on the way home. Its greatest Mustang air victory came when its aircraft were on patrol west of Kassel on March 24, 1945. Several gaggles of Me 109s and FW 190s were engaged and the unit's P-51s destroyed twenty-nine of them. Markings: Spinner from the front banded black, yellow, black and yellow. Black-and-yellow-checkerboard cowling. Sqdn. code letters: 350th-LH, 351st-YJ, 352nd-SX. Top P-51 ace: Lieutenant Colonel W. K. Blickenstaff, 10 victories.

354th Fighter Group: Ninth Air Force. The "Pioneer Mustang" group in the ETO. Began its operations in December 19434. Flew many of its early missions as escort for Eighth AF bombers. The unit's first big victory came on January 5, 1944, when the Mustangs downed eighteen e/a while escorting the bombers to Kiel. Maj.

James H. Howard won the Congressional Medal of Honor for breaking up large enemy fighter force on mission to Halberstadt on January 11, 1944. Moved to France in the summer of 1944 and flew many ground-support as well as fighter-sweep missions. Converted to P-47s for brief period; November 1944-February 1945. Scored over 600 confirmed victories flying Mustangs. Markings: 353rd-White spinners, blue triangles on white noseband. 355th-Blue spinners, blue-and-white-checkerboard noseband. 356th-White spinners, white stars on blue noseband. Sqdn. code letters: 353rd-FT, 355th-GQ, 356th-AJ. Top Score: Lieutenant Colonel G. T. Eagleston. 18.5 victries.

355th Fighter Group: Eighth Air Force. Went operational in Mustangs on March 3, 1944, after flying P-47s. Despite a furious snow squall the unit went down to strafe enemy airdomes on April 5, 1944. In a furious 40-minute attack the P-51s destroyed 43 planes on the ground and shot eight out of the air. Continued to provide bomber escort and to strafe enemy installations until V-E Day. Markings: White spinner and yellow noseband. Sqdn. code letters: 354th-WR, 357th-OS, 358th-YF. Top score: Captain H. W. Brown, 14.2 victories.

356th Fighter Group: Eighth Air Force. Converted to P-51s on November 6, 1944. Flew many combat msisions as escort to the bombers and ground attacks against enemy airfields and installations up to the end of the war. Markings: Red-and-blue-striped spinner bands. Blue diamonds on red cowling. Sqdn. code letters: 359th-OC, 360th-PI, 361st-QI. Top Socre: Lieutenant Colonel D. J. Strait, 13½ victories.

357th Fighter Group: Eighth Air Force. Another group that flew Mustangs from the beginning. Entered operations on February 10, 1944. Received a DUC for their outstanding performance on the first heavy-bomber mission to Berlin on March 6, 1944. The unit tackled terrific enemy opposition, broke up their attacks and downed 20 of them, losing none of their own. On January 14, 1945 the group fought one of the longest and most fierce air battles to take place in the ETO. In a conflict that lasted over thirty minutes the Mustangs downed 56 e/a for a loss of only three P-51s. This unit is credited with 609½ aerial victories. Markings: Spinner from the front banded red, yellow and red. Two red-and-yellow-checkered nosebands. Sqdn. code letters: 362nd-G4, 363rd-B6, 364th-C5. Top score: Major L. K. Carson, 18½ victories.

359th Fighter Group: Eighth Air Force. Converted to P-51s on May 4, 1944. Had an outstanding day while escorting bombers on September 11, 1944. Broke up the attack of 50-plus enemy fighters in the vicinity of Gissen and then went down to engage more fighters taking off from Gotha airdrome. Destroyed five in the air and another four on the ground. Fought off three more gaggles of Luftwaffe fighters attempting to get to the bombers, shooting down more enemy planes. Destroyed seven locomotives on the way home. Total for the day was 35 e/a destroyed in the air and on the ground. Supported the airborne invasion of Holland later that month and flew support missions for the Rhine crossing in March 1945. Markings: Green spinners and cowling. Sqdn. code letters: 368th-CV, 369th-IV, 370th-CS. Top P-51 scorer, Captain Ray S. Wetmore, 17 victories.

361st Fighter Group: Converted to Mustangs on July 28, 1944. Flew many bomber-escort missions. Went to Belgium in December 1944 to fly support during the Battle of the Bulge. Did extensive strafing work in the spring of 1945. Markings: Yellow spinner and noseband. Sqdn. code letters: 374th-B7, 375th-E2, 376th-E9. Top score: Lieutenant D. F. Spencer, 9½ victories.

363rd Fighter Group: Ninth Air Force. Arrived in England in December 1943 and began operations flying Mustangs in January 1944. Flew numerous bomber-escort missions and supported the invasion of France with bombing and strafing missions. Became a tactical reconnaissance group in September 1944. Flew photo- and visual-recce missions up to the end of the war. Sqdn. code letters: 160th-A9, 161st-B3, 162nd-C3. (As fighter squadrons they were designated 380th, 381st and 382nd. Code letters were the same, respectively.) Top scoce: R. J. McWherter, 3 victories.

364th Fighter Group: Eighth Air Force. Converted to P-51s on July 28, 1944. Flew escort, dive-bombing, strafing and patrol missions. Turned in an outstanding performance while escorting the heavies to Frankfurt on December 27, 1944. one squadron attacked gaggles of Greman fighters in the vicinity of Coblenz, shooting down ten of them and breaking up the attack. A second squadron shot down eight out of a gaggle of 15 to 20 FW-190s. The third squadron attacked a formation of 30 FW-190s and destroyed ten of them. Collectively the group had destroyed 28 e/a for the loss of one Mustang. Markings: White spinner. Blue-and-white-striped noseband. Sqdn. code letters: 383rd-N2, 384th-5Y, 385th-5E.

370th Fighter Group: Ninth Air Force. Converted to P-51s in February-March 1945. Bombed bridges and docks in support of the Rhine River crossing. Supported ground operations in the Ruhr Valley. Markings: 401st F.S.-Yellow spinner and horizontal band on vertical tail. 485th F.S.-Red spinner and vertical band on vertical tail. Sqdn. code letters: 401st-7F, 402nd-E6, 485th-9D.

479th Fighter Group: Eighth Air Force. Converted to P-51s on September 27, 1944. Had first big day flying Mustangs on December 5, 1944. Intercepted a big gaggle of German fighters north of Berlin and shot fourteen of them down. On Christmas Day, 1944, the group had three good scraps and downed 23 Luftwaffe fighters. Did excellent strafing work on airfields during March and April 1945. Markings: Natural metal. Squadron colors on rudders only markings used. Squadron code letters: 434th-L2, 435th-J2, 436th-B9.

506th Fighter Group: VII Fighter Command. Flew its first missions from Iwo Jima against the Bonin Islands on May 18, 1945. Participated in several of the VLR escort missions with the B-29s in June of 1945. Markings: 457th F.S.-Red tails. 458th F.S.-Diagonal zebra stripes on tail. 462nd F.S.-Yellow tails. Top score: Captain A. M. Aust, 5 victories.

The 3rd and 5th Fighter Groups of the Chinese-American Composite Wing also operated a number of Mustangs in 1944-45. The exact dates of the P-51 operations are not known.

TOP AAF MUSTANG SCORERS — WORLD WAR II

Name	Unit	P-51 Score	WW II Total	
Maj George E. Preddy	352nd FG	23.83	26.83	3 in P-47
LCol John C. Meyer	352nd FG	21	24	3 in P-47
Capt John J. Voll	31st FG	21	21	
Maj Leonard K. Carson	357th FG	18.50	18.50	
LCol Glenn T. Eagleston	354th FG	18.50	18.50	
LCol John C. Herbst	23rd FG	18	18	
Maj John B. England	357th FG	17.50	17.50	
Maj Robert W. Foy	357th FG	17	17	
Capt James S. Varnell	52nd FG	17	17	
Capt Ray S. Wetmore	359th FG	17	21.25	4.25 in P-47
Capt Don S. Gentile	4th FG	16.50	21.83	5.33 in Spitfire & P-47
Capt Clarence E. Anderson	357th FG	16.25	16.25	
Capt John F. Thornell	352nd FG	16.25	17.25	1 in P-47
Maj Donald M. Beerbower	354th FG	15.50	15.50	
Maj Richard A. Peterson	357th FG	15	15	
LCol Jack T. Bradley	354th FG	15	15	
Maj Samuel J. Brown	31st FG	15	15	
Capt William T. Whisner	352nd FG	14.50	15.50	1 in P-47
Capt. Henry W. Brown	355th FG	14.50	14.50	
Capt Bruce W. Carr	354th FG	14	14	
LCol Edward O. McComas	23rd FG	14	14	

Top P-51 Aces

357th FG	5
352nd FG	4
354th FG	4
23rd FG	2
31st FG	2
4th FG	1
52nd FG	1
355th FG	1
359th FG	1

MUSTANG ACES IN A DAY

Pilot	Unit	Date	Enemy Aircraft
1/Lt C. J. Luksic	352nd FG	May 8, 1944	4 FW-190, 1 Me-109
Maj G. E. Preddy	352nd FG	Aug 6, 1944	6 Me-109
1/Lt W. H. Allen	55th FG	Sep 5, 1944	5 Trainers
1/Lt W. H. Lewis	55th FG	Sep 5, 1944	5 Trainers
1/Lt W. R. Beyer	361st FG	Sep 27, 1944	5 FW-190
Capt C. E. Yeager	357th FG	Oct 22, 1944	5 Me-109
Capt D. S. Bryan	352nd FG	Nov 2, 1944	5 Me-109
1/Lt C. J. Crenshaw	359th FG	Nov 21, 1944	5 FW-190
Capt W. T. Whisner	352nd FG	Nov 21, 1944	5 FW-190
1/Lt J. S. Daniel	339th FG	Nov 26, 1944	5 FW-190
Capt L. K. Carson	357th FG	Nov 27, 1944	5 FW-190
Capt W. J. Hovde	35th FG	Dec 5, 1944	4½ FW-190, 1 Me-109
LCol E. O. McComas	23rd FG	Dec 23, 1944	5 Oscars
Capt E. E. Bankey	364th FG	Dec 27, 1944	4 FW-190, 1½ Me-109
Capt W. A. Shomo	82nd TRS	Jan 11, 1945	6 Tony, 1 Betty
LCol S. S. Woods	4th FG	Mar 22, 1945	5 FW-190
Capt W. Blickenstaff	353rd FG	Mar 24, 1945	3 FW-190, 2-Me-109
Maj R. Elder	353rd FG	Mar 24, 1945	4 FW-190, 1 Me-109
1/Lt B. W. Carr	354th FG	Apr 2, 1945	3 FW-190, 2 Me-109
1/Lt G. W. McDaniel	325th FG	Apr 14, 1945	5 FW-190

By comparison, other USAAF "aces in a day" flew P-47s on nine occasions, P-38s on six missions and P-40s on three.

352nd FG 4
353rd FG 2
357th FG 2
55th FG 2
10 groups 1 each

MUSTANG VICTORIES OVER LUFTWAFFE JETS

4th FG	7 Me-262s, 2 Me-163s, 1 Ar-34	10 Total
20th FG	5½ Me-262s	5½
31st FG	7 Me-262s	7
52nd FG	1 Ar-234	1
55th FG	14 Me-262s, 1 unidentified	15
78th FG	11 Me-262s, 2 Ar-234s	13 (+1 with P-47)
325th FG	1 Me-262	1
332nd FG	3 Me-262s	3
339th FG	14 Me-262s, 2 Ar-234s	16
352nd FG	5½ Me-262s, 2 Ar-234s	7½
353rd FG	6 Me-262s	6 (+1 with P-47)
354th FG	4 Me-262s	4
355th FG	4 Me-262s, 1 Ar-234	5
356th FG	2 Me-262s, 2 Ar-234s	4
357th FG	18 Me-262s	18
359th FG	5 Me-262s, 2 Me-163s	7
361st FG	6 Me-262s	6
364th FG	1½ Me-262s, 1 Me-163	2½
479th FG	5 Me-262s, 1 Ar-234	6

118½ Me-262s, 12 Ar-234s, 5 Me-163s, 1 ? 136½

P-47s were credited with 20½ jets, primarily by the 56th and 365th FGs. Apparently no confirmed jet kills were made by P-38s.

MUSTANG PILOTS CREDITED WITH TWO JETS

Capt D. H. Bochkay	357th FG	2 Me-262s	
Capt G. B. Compton	353rd FG	2 Me-262s	
Capt D. M. Cummings	55th FG	2 Me-262s	(Both Feb 25, 1945)
Capt R. DeLoach	55th FG	2 Me-262s	
1/Lt U. L. Drew	361st FG	2 Me-262s	(Both Oct 7, 1944)
Capt R. S. Fifield	357th FG	2 Me-262s	
Capt N. C. Greer	339th FG	2 Me-262s	
1/Lt H. O. Thompson	479th FG	1 Me-262, 1 Ar-234	

MUSTANGS WITH THE RAF
MARKS I, IA AND II

2 Squadron: Received some of the first Mustangs in mid-1942. Became operational flying photo-reconnaissance missions in November 1942. Flew all three Marks up until mid-November 1944. Sqdn. code letters: XV.

4 Squadron: Received a sprinkling of Mustangs in May 1942 for reconnaissance missions. By early 1943 was largely Mustang equipped. Converted to Spitfires in late 1943. Sqdn. code letters: TV.

16 Squadron: Received first Mustangs in April 1942. Operational with the craft on photo reconnaissance until September 1943. Sqdn. code letters: UG.

26 Squadron: Received Mustangs gradually from February 1942 until operational in July 1942. Flew many missions over the Continent on a series of tours up until late 1943. Operational in Mustang Is again in October 1944, flying many photo missions over V-2 sites in France. Sqdn. code letters: RM, later XC.

63 Squadron: Utilized Mustang I and IAs for many missions over the Continent between June 1943 and February 1944 while assigned to Army Co-operation Command. Sqdn. code letters: NE, later UB.

No. 116 Squadron: Used a few Mustang Is for radar calibration work. No operations.

168 Squadron: Operated Mustang Mark Is and IAs from December 1942 until October 1944. Went to France with Second Tactical Air Force in June 1944 and flew missions from a number of advanced airstrips.

225 Squadron: Borrowed four F-6Bs from USAAF for photo operation during April and May 1943 during the Tunisian campaign.

239 Squadron: Flew Mustangs from May 1942 until October 1943. This unit took part in many photo, recce and strafing operations over occupied Europe during this period. Sqdn. code letters: HB.

169 Squadron: Formed in June 1942 for Mustang intruder operations. Flew many railway and coastal strafing missions, primarily over Holland. Converted to Mosquitoes in late 1943. Sqdn. code letters: VI.

241 Squadron: Received Mustangs in the spring of 1942 but never became operational in them.

260 Squadron: Received a few Mustang Is for transition training in March 1944.

268 Squadron: This tactical-reconnaissance unit utilized some Mustang Mark Is and IAs from June 1942 until the end of the war. Operated from bases in France, Belgium and Hollland late in the conflict. Sqdn. code letters: NM.

309 Squadron: Flew anti-shipping missions utilizing Mustangs from December 1942 until February 1944. Sqdn. code letters: WC.

400 Squadron: This RCAF unit operated some Mustangs on photo-reconnaissance missions from November 1942 until March 1944.

414 Squadron: Received Mustang Is in early summer 1942 and entered combat in August. Scored 1st Mustang victory while covering the Dieppe raid on August 19, 1942. Continued to fly Mustangs until June 1944. Sqdn. code letters: RU.

430 Squadron: Became operational with Mustangs in late May 1943. Flew many missions over France before and during the invasion in 1944. Moved to the Continent in July 1944 and continued to operate Mustang Is until December 1944.

516 Squadron: Formed as a transport squadron in Scotland in April 1943. Operated a few Mustang Is and IAs until early 1944.

613 Squadron: Flew Mustang Is from March 1943 until December 1943. Sqdn. code letters: SY.

MARKS III AND IV

19 Squadron: Mustang operations started in February 1944, with fighter sweeps and escorts to U.S. bombers. Flew numerous anti-shipping escorts. Saw extensive action in support of the Normandy beachhead in June 1944. Moved to France for ground-support duties but returned to U.K. in late September 1944. On September 30, 1944, escorted Lancasters on first daylight mission over the Ruhr. Continued to fly sweeps and escort missions until the end of the war in Europe. Sqdn. code letters: QV.

64 Squadron: Received Mustangs in December 1944 and began flying bomber-escort missions in them at once. Flew cover for numerous Lancaster daylight missions and on January 14, 1945, intercepted and shot down eight enemy aircraft. Sqdn. code letters: SH.

65 Squadron: Flew the first of many escort missions on February 15, 1944. They blooded their Mustangs over Nancy on April 22 and on a sweep to Aalborg, Denmark, heavy enemy opposition was encountered and the Mustangs accounted for nine of them. Began dive bombing in May 1944 and continued this type of ground-support missions during and after the invasion of France. Moved to France on June 26, 1944, and continued to support the Allied armies at various advanced strips up to October 1944. Sqdn. code letters: YT.

118 Squadron: Received Mustangs in December 1944 and began escort operations in February 1945. Flew cover for Lancaster missions until the end of the war. Sqdn. code letters: NK.

112 Squadron: Flew Mark III and IV Mustangs on ground-support operation in Italy from the summer of 1944 until May 1945. Also flew a number of missions over Yugoslavia. Sqdn. code letters: GA.

122 Squadron: began bomber-escort mission flying Mustangs in February 1944. Flew cover for U.S. Bombers to Berlin in March 1944. Caught eight He-111s coming into Dole/Tavaux airfield on April 23, 1944, and shot six of them down. Operated over the invasion area in June 1944 and moved to France late that month. Flew missions in support of ground troops from airstrips on the Continent until September 1944. Did exceptional work during the Arnheim paratroop drop in Holland in September. Became bomber escort until after return to U.K. Sqdn. code letters: MT.

126 Squadron: This unit's Mustangs began escorting the Lancaster bombers in January 1945. While flying cover for the heavies on April 9, 1945, on a mission to the U-boat works at Hamburg, it met and beat off an attack of twelve-plus Me-262 jets, destroying one of them. Sqdn. code letters: 5J.

129 Squadron: Initial Mustang escort operations began in April 1944, but did not see aerial combat until D-day when an FW-190 was shot down. Flew anti-V-1 missions from July until September 1944. Supported the Arnheim operation in September and escorted Lancasters, Halifaxes and Mosquitoes up to the end of the war. Sqdn. code letters: DV.

165 Squadron: Received Mustangs in January 1945 and began bomber-escort operations immediately. Flight Officer Haslops downed an Me-163 while covering the bombers on a mission to Leipzig on April 10, 1945. Sqdn. code letters: SK.

213 Squadron: Received one flight of Mustangs while based in Egypt in June 1944. Fully equipped with Mustangs after move to Italy in July 1944. Flew many missions over Yugoslavia and Greece. Caught He-111s towing Go-242 gliders over Belgrade on September 8, 1944; shot down the two He-111s and destroyed the gliders in the air and on the ground. Flew Mark IIIs and Mark IVs up to the end of the war. Sqdn. code letters: AK.

234 Squadron: Utilized Mustangs for escort missions and fighter sweeps from the fall of 1944 until April 1945. Ended the war escorting Mosquitoes and Beaufighters over Denmark and Norway. Sqdn. code letters: AZ.

249 Squadron: Flew Mustangs with the Balkan Air Force from October 1944 until mid-April 1945. Majority of missions were fighter sweeps and ground strafing over the Balkans and Greece. Sqdn. code letters: GN.

260 Squadron: In mid-March 1944, became the first RAF unit in Italy to receive Mustangs. Flew ground-support and bomber-escort missions to Yugoslavia. In February 1945, began using rockets for ground operations. Sqdn. code letters: HS.

303 Squadron: This Polish unit didn't receive Mustangs until April 1945. Flew a few escort missions in them before V-E. Day. Sqdn. code letters: RF.

306 Squadron: Began flying fighter sweeps in their Mustangs in April 1944. Saw first combat on June 7, 1944, when these Polish pilots tangled with over thirty enemy fighters in the Beuzeville area of France. They destroyed five of the enemy, plus three probables. From late June 1944 until September 1944 the squadron was on anti-V-1 duty. Supported the Arnheim drop over Holland and then resumed escort duties to the end of the war. Squadron Leader J. Zulikowski credited with an Me-262 on April 9, 1945, while escorting Lancasters to Hamburg. Sqdn. code letters: UZ.

309 Squadron: This was another Polish unit which began bomber-escort operations with its Mark III Mustangs in December 1944. While escorting Lancasters to Hamburg on April 9, 1945, it intercepted and beat off an attack from eight Me-262s, destroying three and damaging two of them in the fight. Sqdn. code letters: WC.

315 Squadron: A Polish unit which received its first Mustangs in April 1944. Began bomber-escort missions later the same month. Participated in many bombing and ground-support missions in the invasion area during June 1944. Flew anti-V-1 missions in July 1944. While escorting torpedo Beaufighters on July 30, 1944, encountered 15 enemy fighters and shot down eight of them with no losses. Engaged 60-plus FW-190s in the Beauvais area on August 18, 1944, and shot down sixteen of them, but lost one Mustang — Squadron Leader Horbaczewski. Shot down five enemy fighters on Beaufighter-escort mission to Norway on December 17, 1944. Continued to escort heavy bombers over Germany until the end of the war. Sqdn. code letters: SZ.

316 Squadron: The Mustangs which were received in April 1944, by this Polish squadron were used primarily for convoy patrol up until July 1944, when they went on Anti-V-1 duty. They returned to sea duty in September 1944 and then flew a number of sweeps over Denmark. At the end of October 1944 they began bomber-escort duties for the Lancasters and Halifaxes. Sqdn. code letters: PK.

442 Squadron: Mustang IVs received in April 1945. Flew a few escort missions in the craft before the end of hostilities. Sqdn. code letters: Y2.

611 Squadron: Converted to Mustangs in mid-March 1945. Escorted Lancasters and Halifaxes over Germany until the end of the war. Shot down five FW-190s in the Berlin area on April 16, 1945. Sqdn. code letters: FY.

3 RAAF Squadron: This Italian-based Australian unit operated Mustang Mark IIIs and IVs from November 1944 until V-E Day. The majority of its missions were in ground support in northern Italy and on fighter sweeps over Yugoslavia. Sqdn. code letters: CV.

5 SAAF Squadron: A South African unit which converted to Mustangs in October 1944. Flew ground-support missions from its Italian base up to the end of the war.

LEADING RAF MUSTANG SCORERS

S/Ldr. E. Horbaczewski, DSO, DFC	315 Sqdn.	5.5	16.50	Total
S/Ldr. L. A. P. Burra-Robinson, DFC	122, 65 Sqdns.	5.25	5.25	Total
Sgt. J. Bargielowski, DFM	315 Sqdn.	5	5	Total
S/Ldr. H. Pietrzak, DFC	306, 315 Sqdns.	4.85	7.83	Total
F/O B. Vassiliades, DFM	19 Sqdn.	4.85	7.83	Total
F/Lt. B. G. Collyns, DFC	65, 19 Sqdns.	3.5	8.50	Total
W/Cdr. G. R. A. McG. Johnston, DSO, DFC	122 Wing	3.5	7.50	Total
W/Cdr. W. Christie, DSO, DFC	234 Sqdn.	3	9	Total
S/Ldr. Peter Hearne	19 Sqdn.	3		

LEADING RAF MUSTANG V-1 SCORERS

F/O J. Hartley	129 Sqdn.	11
F/Lt. D. F. Ruchwaldy	129 Sqdn.	10
F/Sgt. S. Rudowski	306 Sqdn.	9.50
F/Sgt. S. Siekierski	306 Sqdn.	9
F/Sgt. J. Zalenski	306 Sqdn.	8.50
W/O T. Szymanski	316 Sqdn.	8
F/Lt. R. G. Kleinmayer	129 Sqdn.	7.50
F/Sgt. A. Pietrzak	315 Sqdn.	7
F/Sgt. T. Jankowski	315 Sqdn.	6.85

FRENCH AIR FORCE

2/33 Tactical Reconnaissance Squadron: Began operations flying F-6C and F-6D aircraft in January of 1945. Did photo survey of the Rhine for French forces. Performed tactical-reconnaissance work for the French First Army after the crossing of the Rhine. Sqdn. code letters: R7.

MUSTANG UNITS IN KOREA

8th Fighter-Bomber Group: August 1950 — December 1950

18th Fighter-Bomber Group: July 1950 — January 1953

35th Fighter-Interceptor Group: July 1950 — May 1951

49th Fighter-Bomber Group: June 1950 — September 1951

67th Tactical Reconnaissance Group operated some RF-51s.

68th Fighter All-Weather Squadron flew F-82s over Korea, June 1950.

339th Fighter All-Weather Squadron operated F-82s over Korea in June 1950.

No. 77 Royal Australian Air Force Squadron flew Mustangs from July 1950 to April 1951.

No. 2 South African Air Force Squadron operated Mustangs from November 1950 to January 1953.

MUSTANG AERIAL VICTORIES IN KOREA

June 27, 1950	1/Lt W. G. Hudson	68th FS	F-82G	Yak-11
June 27	1/Lt R. W. Little	339th FS	F-82G	La-7
June 27	1/Lt C. B. Moran	68th FS	F-82G	La-7
June 29	1/Lt R. J. Burns	35th FS	F-51D	Il-1
June 29	2/Lt O. R. Fox	8th FS	F-51D	Il-1
June 29	1/Lt H. T. Sandlin	8th FS	F-51D	La-7
Aug. 3	Capt E. C. Hoagland	67th FS	F-51D	Yak
Nov. 1	Capt R. D. Thresher	67th FS	F-51D	Yak-3
Nov. 1	Capt A. R. Flake	67th FS	F-51D	Yak-3
Nov. 2	Capt A. R. Flake	67th FS	F-51D	Yak-9
Nov. 2	1/Lt J. L. Glessner	12th FS	F-51D	Yak-9
Nov. 6	Capt H. I. Price	67th FS	F-51D	1½Yak-9
Nov. 6	1/Lt H. S. Reynolds	67th FS	F-51D	½Yak-9
Feb. 5, 1951	Major A. Mullins	67th FS	F-51D	Yak-9
June 20	1/Lt J. B. Harrison	67th FS	F-51D	Yak-9

INDEX